Seminar Proceedings No. 29

CULTURE IN AFRICA
AN APPEAL FOR PLURALISM

Edited by
Raoul Granqvist

Nordiska Afrikainstitutet, Uppsala, 1993
(The Scandinavian Institute of African Studies)

Indexing terms
Communication
Culture
Literature
Popular culture
Africa

Cover picture: Anna Bengtsson
Copyediting: Sonja Johansson
Language polishing: Raoul Granqvist and Tony Huzzard

© Nordiska Afrikainstitutet, 1993

Printed in Sweden by
Bohusläningens Boktryckeri AB, Uddevalla 1993

ISSN 0281-0018
ISBN 91-7106-330-7

Contents

Introduction: African Culture—an Estimate

Raoul Granqvist

Theoreticians in the field of cultural studies claim that any cultural study is by necessity linked to the study of social structures. Jeffrey C. Alexander has pointed out that an agreement between these two concepts is fundamental.

> We cannot understand culture without reference to subjective meaning, and we cannot understand it without reference to social structure constraints. We cannot interpret social behavior without acknowledging that it follows codes that it does not invent; at the same time human invention creates a changing environment for every cultural code.[1]

Wole Soyinka, although writing from another perspective, seems to agree. He also discriminates between social structure and the human construct, but claims that the latter aspect has been harmfully politicized in the African context. In a speech called "The African World and the Ethnocultural Debate," which he gave in Lagos at a conference to discuss the Festival of Black and African Culture in 1977, he derides the "ideologist" who always "plumbs for its [the rain's] economic primacy, [and] reduces its interaction with society purely to the organization of agricultural and marketing science and around the appearance, regularity, or uncertainty of rainfall." Knowledge about the "affective outlook," as he calls the human interaction with its material and symbolic environment, is particularly essential, he insists, in a post-colonial situation which must combat self-denial.[2]

Soyinka is not only trying to find a balance between the two, but raise the value and significance of the "affective outlook." In other words it is in the landscape informed by a dialectic of the "subjective

---

1. Jeffrey C. Alexander, "Analytic debates: Understanding the relative autonomy of culture," in *Culture and Society: Contemporary Debates*, ed. Jeffrey C. Alexander and Steven Seidman (New York, Port Chester, Melbourne, Sydney: Cambridge University Press, 1990) 26.

2. Wole Soyinka, "The African World and the Ethnocultural Debate," in *African Culture: The Rhythms of Unity*, ed. Molefi Kete Asante and Kariamu Welsh Asante (Trenton, N. J., Africa World Press) 33 and 34.

meaning" and the concomitant and complementary "social structure," of the individual experience and the circumscribing social institution, of the chat about whether we will have rain tomorrow and
the weather forecasts on the radio or TV, that we, according to him,
should focus our attention. In Soyinka's dicta we recognize the
agents of a continuum of experience, the layering of interactions and
symbolic practices that link us as individuals with the history and
the society of a distinct place, whether it be in Africa or in northern
Europe.

Narrowing our focus on African culture further we discover that
Soyinka, and many with him, claims that there exists a common
bond that transcends the experiences of the black race across the
continents, linking Africa with parts of the Americas and the
Caribbean. These are what he calls the "enia dudu," a Youruba expression for "the black peoples," linked by a common tragic heritage
of victimization, forceful emigration, ideological and human denigration, but also of complementarity, interaction and productivity.[3]
Soyinka's standpoint is illuminated by, what one perhaps could describe as, faith in "combatant, comparative universalism" and a non-
exclusive ethnocultural reality. Molefi Kete develops this view further and also, I believe, distorts it. In his essay "Afrocentricty and
Culture," in the book *African Culture: The Rhythms of Unity*, Kete
explains:

> African culture is … determined by a unity of origin as well as a common
> struggle. All of the African people who participated in the mechanized interac-
> tion with Europe, and who colored the character of Europe while being
> changed themselves, share a commonality. Also present in African culture is a
> nonmaterial element of resistance to the assault upon traditional values ….[4]

Soyinka would largely agree with this analysis but hardly when Kete
explains, without reservations, that "African culture takes the view
that an Afrocentric modernization process would be based upon
three traditional values: harmony with nature, humaneness, and
rhythm."[5] It is *not* that Jahnheinz Jahn's philosophical triad
"harmony with nature, humaness, and rhythm," which he has bor-
rowed, may not be a qualitative, and even a normative, trope for

---

3. Soyinka 16.

4. *African Culture: The Rhythms of Unity* 6.

5. *Ibid.* 7.

African society, it is that Kete has made it *exclusive*. This parochialism is carried out by the book project itself, which provides little space for alternative models. The African dance, the oral tale, the unsigned painting, the curvilinear movement, the actual and the past, the secular and the divine operate, it must be understood, reciprocally and complementarily as part of a "grand total" or a non-unified system. So what is disturbing is that African cultural productions, defined as exclusive, are prevented from communicating and reciprocating with the outsider, not out of any conspiracy of their own, but out of a conspiracy of a particular cultural critique's standpoint. It is the idea of advocating cultural closure that we should challenge. Afrocentricity as it is *not defined* by the book *African Culture: The Rhythms of Unity* is a valid and useful concept; in the way it *is defined* and performed it is irrelevant.[6]

That western critical discourse on Africa for centuries has been jaundiced and imperial is a statement that needs no corroboration here. The denigration of her cultural productions through misquotations and misrepresentations has been monumental. Western hierarchical notions of literary categories and canononical preferences have tended to obscure the artefacts under consideration. "Universality," says James Snead, to take one of the most favoured western designations, "seems often merely to function as a codeword meaning 'comprehensibility for the European reader.'"[7] This concept and its presumptions are actually the only real constants in the winding history of western reception of African through patterns, ranging from

---

6. Unfortunately this exclusivity is becoming more and more a marker of Afro-American criticism, even to the point of establishing race-centred antagonisms within the academies. It is noticeable in American criticism where there is an ongoing tug of war between academics on issues of the "whiteness" and "blackness" that to me comes close to paranoia, on both sides of the pigmentation. See, i.e., Michael Awkward's article "Negotiations of Power: White Critics, Black Texts, and the Self-Referential Impulse," *American Literary History*, 2.4 (1990): 581–606. See also the editorial in *The New Republic* (February 1991)—a special edition on "race in the campus"—that explains that "'multiculturalism' turns out ... to be neither multi nor cultural. In practice, its objective is a unanimity of thought on campus that, if successful, would effectively end open exchange—exchange that would have to include the alleged representatives of patriarchy—and reduce the nuances of culture to the determinants of race (6)."

7. James Snead, "European pedigrees/African contagions: nationality, narrative, and communality in Tutuola, Achebe, and Reed," in *Nation and Narration*, ed. Homi K. Bhabha (London and New York: Routledge, 1990) 237.

the travelogues of the eighteenth century disciples of Carl von Linné
to the twentieth century commentaries of African novels.

So whether we are are dealing with Afrocentrism or Eurocentrism,
in the manner I have prejudiced them, they are equally stifling, re-
ductive and reactionary, Afrocentrism because it expels and silences,
Eurocentrism because it seeks to dominate the other. For the
emergent African text, that is, for African culture, to open up, to become, if not transparent but visible, and move from the margin to its
own centre and to the centre of world attention, and back again, we
need to perform a number of challenging negotiations with it.

These negotiations can indeed be manifold: functionalist, semiotic,
dramaturgical, weberian, durkheimian, marxian, feminist, poststruc-
turalist and so on. An accompanying list of names of protagonists of
such orientations would include: Wilhelm Dilthey, Antonio Gramsci,
Roland Barthes, Erving Goffman, Michael Weber, Victor Turner, Paul
Willis, Michel Foucault, Jean-François Lyotard, Jürgen Habermas,
Edward Said. But the main question is can any of these approaches
to cultural studies be applied on African experiences, African cultures, despite their obvious different regional and socio-economic
ancestry? Can we indiscriminately use any western oriented scientific approach to find answers about a reality with which there is
little synchronism? The premise for these questions is the understanding that it is not very relevant to ask somebody in northern
Scandinavia, in February, whether it will rain tomorrow; the
question may be as absurd as asking a Nigerian whether he/she
believes in the government or the more neutral question whether
he/she speaks only English. All the questions in the world, asked or
not, as all literary and scientific theories and interpretations, are part
of a culture and thus self-reflexive. Indeed

> ... every theoretical conception of culture is itself a form of cultural activity, and
> ... every concrete act of interpretation will not only be implicated in the back-
> ground of cultural practices which has formed the interpreters but will also de-
> velop or counter the implicit self-conception of that cultural background. In this
> sense, interpretations are caught up in a process of self-understanding or self-
> misunderstanding even as they engage an object or text to be understood. ...
> [S]uch processes of hermeneutical self-understanding/self-misunderstanding
> are also bound up with the conflicting self-understandings of a society that is

divided by its institutionalized relations of domination, coercion, and exploitation.[8]

This hermeneutical model would then exclude most, if not all, of the critical approaches listed above, as applicable to explore an African experience, as they are reflections and extensions of western theoretical thinking and western social realities and traditions. However, a dismissal on such unilateral grounds seems to me unimaginable and unresourceful.

The proviso is, however, that they are allowed to be mitigated, modified, revised or, indeed, "de-colonized," if the specificity of the context that they are applied to so requires. In this sense, *any* interpretive strategy can become useful when subjected to a demobilizing or appropriating process. One is reminded of Chinua Achebe's saying that the ultimate choice for the African writer is not whether to write in English or in an African language, it is what you do with your language that matters.

This book advances then the position that no specific thinking and inquiry into African cultural matters is self-sufficient and that it should be based on an interplay of influences. African cultural studies invite the tolerance of the metonymy. The book includes not only a great variety of subjects but also a medley of associative methodologies. The objective is to broaden the perspective of what we normally mean by African culture and approaches to such culture and to confront or challenge the tendency towards essentialism or alienation.

The book underscores the need for a broader acceptance of critical thinking and a concomitant rejection of hypocritical shunning of daring and incongruent constellations of theorizing about Africa. The flow of ideas and theories is a criss-crossing movement. To give one example, Henry Louis Gates, Jr., the foremost spokesman for self-generated theories about black traditions, has advanced this field in a few American academies. However, his work has begun to play a role outside their primacy; black text-specific theories are influential also outside the parameters of the "black" text.

It is the possibilities and potentialities of the particular work that the different reading strategies must try to explore and deconstruct.

---

8. John Brenkman, *Culture and Domination* (Ithaca and London: Cornell University Press, 1987) 5.

And they should be free to do so, in whatever wild, but text-explo-rative manner. Any attempt to circumscribe this endeavour by atti-tudinal projects emanating from different -isms or centres will even-tually strike back on its advocate. African culture may be a mis-nomer, but learning about it humbly and intelligently is to break si-lences, our own and that of others, and to add new sounds and signs to the endless chart that embodies the human enterprise.

"I look forward to an African leader whom I can meet in the street, with a loaf of well-priced bread under my arm, to challenge him on his budget speech the previous day, while he challenges me on the literary merit of my latest bad novel or poem." This politico-cultural credo by the Zimbabwean writer Chenjerai Hove, from one of the es-says in this book, is an aspiration that cultural workers everywhere in the world are likely to embrace. It epitomizes the essence of any cultural strategy worthy of the name. It postulates freedom of ex-pression and suppression of freedom as its antithetical frames of ref-erence. It engages voices of dissonance and multiplicity and rallies speakers from different compartments of life who—ideally at least—are equal.

In this sense cultural practices and the studies of them should be universal. Yet African cultural studies have been particularly slow to develop. No doubt, one reason for this is the ideological coercion they occasionally are subject to and that Hove alludes to in his state-ment. Another reason is, we saw, the very nature of the western scientific discourse that may compartmentalize rather than liberate. The literary scholar or the anthropologist, to mention only two actors on the African scientific scene, have seldom been able to join hands and share critically their observations. However such pursuits are now becoming legitimate and honourable. Here we offer one.

The first three essays of the book deal with Zimbabwe. The first chapter written by the ethnomusicologist *Olof Axelsson* explores Zimbabwean church music drama. Axelsson's objective is to study how the acculturation process in post World War II Zimbabwe has affected the Shona traditions of singing and telling with particular relevance to the mechanisms of the proverb (*tsumo*) and the story (*ngano*). Through an extensive analysis of two such church dramas *Mazuva ekupedzisa*, based on the Christian Passion story, and *Mweya waMwari*, on pieces from the Old and New testaments and late 1970s Zimbabwean history, Axelsson demonstrates how the intermingling of genres (oral, narrative, music, drama, hymnology etc.) and cultural traditions (Shona and western) can contribute to the moulding of experiences that are imperative for a dynamic people's culture.

Hilde Arntsen and *Knut Lundby* are conducting research into the impact of religious broadcasting on African culture. More specifically they present in their chapter some preliminary obeservations of how Zimbabwe students respond to the international version of Pat Robertson's "electronic church" propaganda. The fact that the students seem to discard the intended message of the communication and appropriate it to suit their own "readings" lead the two writers to conclude that there is little risk of an immediate media imperialism in Africa, although the tension it produces is imperative in the positioning of power in the cultural process.

The essay by *Chenjerai Hove*, is a vituperant attack on the African one-party state and the arrogance of its traditionally self-appointed leadership. This small essay has previously been printed by *Index of Censorship* (6: 1991).

The fourth essay, written by two linguists, *Lars-Gunnar Andersson* and *Tore Janson* is concerned about languages in Botswana, their functionality and status. Andersson and Janson organize the languages of Botswana along the parameter of poor-developing-rich, with Setswana, the language of the majority (80 per cent of the population), as occupying the mediating position in the linguistic triad. The developing features of a language, the writers suggest, can be tested—as well as advanced—within three areas: its linguistic competence (availability of grammars, dictionaries, well-functioning ortographies etc), the literary aspect (there is no novel yet in Setswana!), and education (Setswana is the language of instruction only for the first four years). Setswana is well on its way to becoming, the writers prophesy, a *rich* language. But, one could ask, would this "development" simultaneously be a death blow to Botswana's twenty "real" minority languages?

The departure of *Bodil Folke Frederiksen's* examination of Kenyan popular literature is the assumption that this genre—perhaps better than any other—embodies and articulates cultural changes involving class, ethnicity, gender, and age. Her study is focussed on a number of Kenyan popular novels and the magazine *Joe* where, in her terminology, "the ordinary is the utopia"; humdrum urban realism (in a western sense) has been turned into a fantastic world of make-believe where the protagonists act out their dreams and frustrations. But this literature, Frederiksen points out, also functions (perhaps less now than in the 1970s) as a socializing and educating agent, quick to respond to the communication process at hand.

Illiteracy does not equal literary incompetence. This is proved yet again by *Ingrid Björkman*'s chapter on the orature aspects of Kenyan women's literature. By applying Vladimir Propp's theories of the morphology of the folktale on a story by Grace Ogot and a folk tale from the Rift Valley province and projecting these narratives and a couple of others to two women's groups of recipients—one consisting of illiterate peasant women, the other of middle class urban women—Björkman shows that the oral traditions are very influential in moulding modern writing but, above all, that the interpretive communities, the societies of norm-guiding or norm-breaking women, appropriate stories and tales to serve their own purposes that may either involve self-denial or liberation.

Taking his main example from Kolo Omotoso's *The Edifice*, the English-Nigerian writer *Adewale Maja-Pearce* castigates in his essay African writers for romanticising Africa and ignoring, out of artistic inability or sheer unwillingness, the complexity of the African heritage with its modern European components. The pluralism of Africa, he implies, has been too little exploited by the African writers themselves.

In her essay on Islamic architecture and art, richly illustrated, *Karin Ådahl* draws attention to the lack of research into the area, despite the lasting impact they have exercised on the cultures of both sub-Saharan Africa and North Africa. Is Islamic art different from African art in general? she asks. Or is it that the interaction over the regions makes this question superfluous? Her own survey of Mali architecture demonstrates tentatively a communality of conceptions and techniques that, she suggests, need to be examined with much more scholarly rigour.

The next chapter concerns Nigeria from the inside—by an informed outsider. *Kacke Götrick* writes about the sequential pattern of Yoruba theatre where the traditional function of the actor vacillates between the non-mimetic and the mimetic with liminality as its dramatic core. The Gelede Society priest-actor is then able to cross the boundary between the human and the superhuman realm and bring messages to this world; Götrick describes his double function as fictional and religious liminality. She then explores the degree of liminality in a modern drama, Obotunde Ijimere's (a pen name for Ulli Beier) *The Imprisonment of Obatala* and suggests that its operational stretch is dependent on, and complicated by, at least two things: the "ritual" competence shared by the audience and the actors and the relationship of the theatrical event with the traditions of the print version of the play.

Gillian Stead Eilersen's chapter on Bessie Head is a well-rounded sketch of Eilersen's forthcoming biography of the writer. She examines Head's search for her roots and identity through observations of her novels and writings, pays particular attention to her family background as a social outcast and a child of a white mother and a black father, and confronts the assumption that Head herself created a biographical legend. In a final note, Eilersen adds an ideological interpretation to Head's search for a "frame of reference," explaining that by "her struggle to establish an identity for herself ... she has also offered to all those who live on the continent of Africa the chance of a greater self-awareness and self-respect."

Carl F. Hallencreutz discusses the cultural/political appropriation of the legacy of King Shaka and Dingane by different leaderships in the South African liberation struggle, with Nelson Mandela opting for Dingane, Albert Luthuli and Mazisi Kunene, the Zulu poet, for Shaka, and Thomas Mofolo, the novelist and writer of *Chaka*, placing himself between the two groups in projecting Shaka as cruel and imperial. Hallencreutz finally points to a sensitive dilemma: the adoption of the Shaka tradition and its praise poetry (*izibongo*) by the Inkatha movement and Mongosuthu Buthelezi.

Another South African dilemma is how far indigenous writing should be involved with the struggle or whether such a literary programmatic is valid at all; if one should hail to Nadine Gordimer's (perhaps) idealistic prerogative that the writer should "tell the truth as he sees it in his own words without being accused of letting the side down." *Rose Petterson* claims in her examination of the character Liz van Den Sandt in *The Late Bourgeois World* that Gordimer is not wholly true to her conviction: there is a discord in the character Liz, as well as in Gordimer's own text. A "propagandistic standard" has crept in.

Christian Poetry and Music Drama: Black Cultural Expression in Zimbabwe

Olof Axelsson

> Don't close the window
>   or curtain it,
> For Africa speaks outside:
> The spatter of raindrops on the heart
>   sings eternal songs:
> Would my drummer were here.
>
> (from Chenjerai Hove, *Up in Arms*,
> Harare: Zimbabwe Publishing House, 1982)

There has been a dynamic surge for Black cultural expression within the Christian churches in Zimbabwe since the decades around World War II. The aim of my presentation is to throw some light on a number of questions regarding the music traditions and acculturation processes of the Shona people within such an environment. The most conspicuous aspect is the continuous emergence of new church music in which Black traditional ideas and western concepts intermingle in a fascinating manner giving rise to questions of origin. Alongside this "fresh" and inspiring development, western traditional hymnody continues to be at work in the different denominations, some of it appearing more or less "untouched" and static, while some is exposed to constant change and expansion.

Since the commencement in the early 1950s of such dynamic church music activitites, new—or transformed—forms and genres have emerged. Some of them have prevailed, whereas others have had a short, but intensive life.[1] To the latter belongs a genre mostly known in Zimbabwe as *church music opera*. In this genre different art

---

1. The explanation for such a diverse process possibly lies in a combination of different factors. The most important ones seem to be that a) literate and musical material have been disseminated through the medium of *oral tradition*—in some cases combined with cyclostyled textsheets; b) the relationship between content and Christian/social situations is no longer relevant—or of less importance; and c) selective attitudes seem to have been at work through individuals or groups actively involved in church work.

forms exist side by by side; expressive drama and dance appear in conjunction with poetry and music. It is an artistic form and activity in which various Black traditional concepts assimilate elements from without—or combine with them—in different degrees. Such musical plays mainly deal with the major festivities within the Christian calendar year: Christmas, Passiontide, and Easter.

In this analysis of two church music dramas I will examine poetic structures built on traditional forms and their transformation into musical forms. I will look into the traditional forms of certain musical and poetical characteristics and point out some acculturation aspects in this process. Which aspects may be referred to as specific and genuine Shona poetic structures? How are such structures used in music? Is it possible to find assimilation tendencies, particularly emanating from the western Christian churches? To what extent and in what manner are acculturation processes at work? And finally, which traditional Shona genres serve as the main inspirational background? Thus the point of departure is the relationship between text and music.

Certain characteristics appear to point to a close relationship between the rhythm of the spoken language and its transformation into a rhythmic musical context. This issue has been much discussed but so far no final conclusions have been reached. Akwabena Nketia, Robert Kaufmann, James Koetting and Rose Brandel among others have touched upon the matter, and particularly Nketia has been successful in his comparison of the Akan language and its music.[2] Gerhard Kubik, one of the most outstanding ethnomusicologists on the African scene, has emphasized the close relationship between verbal and musical rhythm and pointed out the relevance of the tonal patterns in melodic structures of cultural areas where so-called tonal languages are the common denominator.[3] In his comparative analysis of Shona traditional poetry, George Fortune has outlined its phonological structure stating that it is not constructed along stress

---

2. Kwabena J.H. Nketia, *The Music of Africa* (London: Victor Gollanz, 1975); Robert Kauffman, "African Rhythm: A Reassessment," *Ethnomusicology* 24.3 (1980): 393–415; Rose Brandel, *The Music of Central Africa: An Ethnomusicological Study* (The Hague: Martinus Nijhoff, 1961); James Koetting, "What Do We Know About African Rhythm?," *Ethnomusicology* 30.1: 58–63.
3. Gerhard Kubik, "Musikgestaltung in Afrika," *Musik in Afrika,* ed. Artur Simon (Berlin 1983) 27–40.

language patterns.[4] A linguist in Southern Africa E. Westphal noted as early as 1948 that "linguistic stress seems to coincide with musical stress and it seems that the change of words brings about the cross-rhythm in singing."[5]

In a number of hypotheses about different aspects of structures in African rhythm, terms like *divisive, additive* and *hemiola* are often referred to. In comparing language rhythm and musical rhythm the question arises as to whether it is possible to speak about an *additive language pattern* which determines—or at least has an effect on—the additive aspects in the musical process. This question has, as far as I know, not yet been posed. Nonetheless, such an investigation could certainly present a number of fascinating aspects.

The question of what kind of messages are communicated is also an important aspect. Are, for example, theological concepts related to present situations? Are these music dramas purely musical and dramatic entertainment, or do they serve specific functions in society? How are Christian aspects related to traditional religious aspects? My analysis will point towards the hypothesis that in spite of western influence the artistic and creative processes of contemporary Black church music in Zimbabwe follow specific indigenous patterns.

The material

This paper concerns two musical plays. The first one is *Mazuva ekupedzisa* written and composed by Abraham Dumisani Maraire in 1965. It is a dramatic and musical interpretation of the Passion Story covering some of the most known events in the latter part of the life of Jesus, and particularly his last week on earth—from Palm Sunday to Maundy Thursday, Good Friday and Easter Sunday. The play ends with the astounding event of some women and disciples finding the tomb empty. Basing their belief on the words of Jesus, who had already foretold his death and resurrection, they proclaimed that a miracle had occurred *"Aleluya, Jesu wedu wamuka!"* (Alleluia, our

---

4. George Fortune, "Shona Traditional Poetry," *Zambezia* 2.1 (1971): 42.
5. E. Westphal, "Linguistics and the African Music Research," *African Music Society Newsletter* 1.1 (1948): 15.

Jesus is arisen). Hence the title which simply means "The Last Days."[6]

Apart from the LP disc (see footnote 6) there is a cyclostyled version with the same title containing the complete text. The printed version holds a few very sparse comments about stage action. However, there are no indications as to *where* the play is supposed to be performed and the few notes about its first performances do not specify whether it was performed in a church setting or outdoors. In the cyclostyled AACMA (All-Africa Church Music Association) journal a reference is made to the play:

> The Holy Week musical play of Abraham Maraire, which is called Mazuva Ekupedzisa (The Last Days), has been a great success. Students of the Nyadiri Teacher Training School performed it well under the direction of Mr. Maraire, and it was enthusiastically received in Salisbury [Harare] and Umtali [Mutare] as well as at Nyadiri. Mr. Maraire has also written a Christmas musical play, which will begin to be rehearsed soon. (3.2 [1965]: 11)

Verbal information from a close associate of the composer and director Patrick Matsikenyiri indicates that the performances took place outdoors as well as indoors (in churches and church assembly halls) and that no props or stage scenery were used. Changes of scene were indicated by direct physical relocations within a decided acting area.

After its performances in 1965 the play was not set up again until 1974. This time it was staged in Bulawayo in the southern part of the country. Together with students at Kwanongoma College of Music and teacher students of the United College of Education I brought it back into performance, now within the compass of the liturgical church calender. The play had its debut in the Anglican Cathedral of Bulawayo on Palm Sunday evening 10th April 1974 in front of a multi-cultural audience. It was then performed on two occasions during Holy Week in two other churches in the city (on 11th and 12th April). Since its debut in Bulawayo the play was performed annually until 1978 during this particular time of the Church calendar.

The second church music drama that I will consider derives its inspiration from different stories in the Old and New testaments of the Bible, particularly the concepts dealing with the spirit of God and how it may affect the individual and/or the collective in society, i.e.

---

6. Abraham Maraire, "Mazuva ekupedziza" (An African Holy Week Cantata), *Umbowo Records*, Church Music Service, P.B. 636 E, Harare, 1966.

God's People. Hence the title, *Mweya waMwari—The Spirit of God.*[7] It differs from the former play in that the creative activities that it entails were shared by a number of people. Furthermore, the content does not, as is the case in *Mazuva*, include a particular story. Instead, it centres on a number of events that were relevant to the historical and political situation of Zimbabwe in the late 1970s, such as the devastating effects the armed struggle for independence and freedom had on the local people. After the structure of the play had been worked out by a handful of people it was presented to three poets/musicians who composed both the poetic texts based on biblical references and the music. They were Patrick Matsikenyiri, John Nduna, and Julius Mushuku, well-known musicians and choir leaders in Zimbabwe.

Shona traditional poetry—a brief outline of genres

In order to make an intelligible comparison between Shona traditional poetry and music based on vocal presentation, it is necessary to outline some of the main forms. They consist of proverbs, riddles, fancy stories, and traditional poetry. In the Shona language the terms are *tsumo (shumo)*, *chipare*, *ngano* and *nhetembwa* respectively.[8] In this context I will only deal with *tsumo* (proverbs) and *ngano* (fancy stories).

I am unable, neither is it necessary, to present a more thorough analysis of *tsumo* (proverbs) or *ngano* (tale; fancy story; sing. *rungano*) in the traditional Shona context. Suffice it to mention that both genres represent age-old wisdom from which human and social behaviour and attitudes take their inspiration. Even in the modern and materialistic world of today these genres play an important role in daily life, both through the traditional forms and their uses in modern literature and poetry.

Considering the oral art of Shona, its verbal structure often contains only one sentence which is usually divided into two parts (indicated in vocal presentation by a well-defined pause). The verbal content is highly condensed, rich in associations, and very expressive.

---

7. "Vibrant Zimbabwe" Sacred and Secular Music from Kwanongoma College of Music; *LP record PROP 7808*, Proprius Musik AB, Stockholm, Sweden, 1979.
8. See Fortune, "Shona Traditional Poetry," *Zambezia* 2.1 (1971): 41–60.

Tsumo -proverbs

Chemberi masikati/	An old woman during day/
usiku imvana	at night a young mother
Imbwa payaduira/	The place where the dog has fed/
haipakanganwi	it does not forget
Chidembo hachinzwi/	The polecat does not smell/
kunhuwha kwacho	its own stink.[9]

Verbal delivery is of great importance whether the presentation concerns a proverb or a story. Such expressivity is received through well-defined structural differences in the relative tonal treatment of the voice. The initial vocal attack commences from the upper register of the voice and gradually slides down to the middle section of the first phrase—the middle *cadenza*. The second part of the sentence follows the same overall structure ending with the final *cadenza*, but now at a slightly lower level. It is actually possible to talk about two different tonal levels in speech, each comprising an ambiguous intervallic distance; usually anything between a third to a fifth. Within each tonal area, sliding effects are noticeable and are guided by the inherent tonal inflections of syllables and their combinations into lexical units. Furthermore, the two tonal levels are roughly a tone or more apart with a rather apparent tonal relationship to each other. A graphic illustration could take this shape:

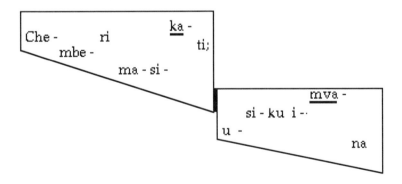

---

9. The examples of proverbs above have been taken from: *Tsumo—Shumo: Shona Proverbial Lore and Wisdom*, ed. Mordikai A. Hamutyinei and Albert B. Plangger (Gweru: Mambo Press, 1974).

The length and structure of the text holds natural limits which—at this stage of presentation—correspond to a "hidden" melodic and rhythmic phrase. Then the question arises as to whether the text itself is additive in its lexical and poetic form in a manner similar to that of the musical line. With the assistance of grammatical changes, but carrying similar lexical content, as well as with that of adding vocables (verbal expressions without direct lexical meaning), such a manner of approach seems possible to adopt.

The Shona language can be characterized as holding components or "building blocks." Through a combination of either a single, or a combined consonant sound (C +[exp.]), and immediately followed by a vowel sound (V), such a component constitutes a morpheme or syllable. By the addition of components, meaningful verbal units are created. Hence all meaningful units,   words, or combinations of words in larger units, end on a vowel. A rhyming structure similar to the English "strong" rhymes cannot therefore be used in Shona.[10] The first and second proverbs above would then be structured:

Che-   mbe- ri   ma- si- ka- ti;   u - si- ku   i -   mva- na
[C^2V + C^2V +CV+ CV+CV+CV+CV;   V + CV+ CV+V + C^2V + CV]

I -   mbwa pa- ya- du- i- ra;   ha- i- pa- ka- nga- nwi
[V + C^3V + CV+CV+CV+V+CV;   CV+V+ CV+CV +C^2V + C^2V]

On the next structural level, consideration must be given to the length of the syllables and units. Well-known is the fact that the Shona language places a lengthening on the penultimate syllable of a phrase. However, also within the phrase, different syllables receive different *time space*—an issue which has not been dealt with to any great degree apart from analytical and interesting thoughts expressed by Nketia.[11] Within such differences in time space, certain important aspects of musical rhythmic structures may be found—a hypothesis well worth investigating further through the co-operation between linguistic and musicological teamwork. Again, in simplistic terms it is possible to distinguish between short syllabic units and units roughly double and triple in length. Applying musical note values to a rhythmic graph of above proverbs it is possible to use the

---

10. *Ibid.* 42.
11. Nketia, *The Music of Africa* 177 ff.

quaver 𝅘𝅥𝅮 to respresent a short sound and a *crotchet* 𝅘𝅥 to indicate the double length sound.

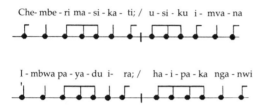

The rhythmic structure is always correctly expressed in a spoken presentation. However, in the musical context there might occur situations when a "rhythmic game" seems to be produced, i.e. word structures are treated in an opposite manner to the spoken equivalent and hence create rhythmic flavours and intricacies which serve as an additional enhancement of the understanding of the text. Verbal/rhythmic "turns" of such a nature are often visually expressed in facial and bodily gestures resulting in dance.

In the early 1970s I worked with one of the most outstanding and well-known musicians and church music composers in Zimbabwe, Patrick Matsikenyiri. Our intention was to produce a simple and comprehensive guide to the basics of western staff notation, particularly to be used by teachers and other church workers interested in music. At Matsikenyiri's suggestion we decided to go through a number of short and common verbal phrases of types similar to proverbs and riddles with the idea of using them as basic illustrations for musical pitch and duration. After having collected well over a hundred expressions supposedly known and used by children in their games, fifty-one sayings were selected by Matsikenyiri. The procedure adhered to was to establish the verbal rhythmic flow and illustrate it with the durational note values of *quaver* and *crotchet*. I then transcribed the readings of Matsikenyiri in rhythmic patterns. Then he spontaneously sang the sayings to the rhythm. In the production of these melodies we adhered to the tonal inflections provided by speech. The melodies were then transcribed.

The following two phrases appear as nos. 15 and 16:

Pote pote sakariende   Back, back; that's why it is gone
Tsare wako kadeyadeya   Pick your partner and play

The rhythmic and melodic structure received the following form:

Spoken rhytm   Spoken rhytm

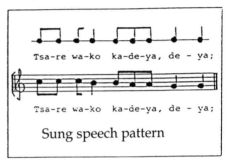

Sung speech pattern   Sung speech pattern

Slightly changed both sayings look like traditional songs; the first one is a worksong patterned on a typical leader-response form and dealing with the dreariness of hard work.

The Shona song "Sekeriende"

The second one is a children's song teaching correct courting manners.

The Shona song "Saura wako"

Comparing Matsikenyiri's short melodic phrases with the two songs it is clear that they share the same rhythmic flow. Also, the melodic movements in them are of the same kind: they are inscribed by tonal inflections. And thirdly, the two songs are short and based on repetition; a structure which corresponds to that of the proverb.[12] Short poetic and musical structures are easy to memorize.

An additional concept of reciprocity exists in the well-known and ubiquitous structure of antiphonal singing and music-making in Africa, the manner described as the "call and response pattern." Including recently composed church music and popular music, Shona music as a whole is recognised by its antiphonal or responsorial character. Shona traditional poetry could also be characterized as

---

12. Fortune, "Shona Traditional Poetry," *Zambezia* 2.1 (1971).

responsorial; its bipartite structure lends itself easily to a responsorial presentation.

Although both Shona proverbs and riddles have this formal structure, it is most conspicuous in the genre of *ngano* (sing. *rungano;* story-telling). Regarded as a waning traditional activity, it is nevertheless common in the rural areas of Zimbabwe where daily life centres around tilling the lands and coming together at the evening fires for entertainment. Whereas the genre of *tsumo* involves an individual addressing a group in normal speech, intertwined with words of wisdom, the *ngano* involves group participation. This is achieved through the "collective" response that follows almost each phrase by the storyteller. The response consists of only one word—*dzepfunde*—and apparently acts as a means of increasing intensity and drama in the story. Hence, the storyteller is prompted to produce an even higher level of expression as the story proceeds. The performance usually also evokes singing seemingly on the spur of the moment, although the content of the song would be previously known, at least as a kind of a musical formula. This storytelling also increases the activity and curiosity on the part of the listeners-participants. The root meaning of *pfunde* is connected with plants or grain,[13] possibly an implicit idea of growth when applied to denote the story as *dzepfunde.*

A particular *rungano* does not carry the same order of text—even content may be changed depending on the personality of the narrator. It is not a particular text learnt by rote that is to be reproduced the same way every time; rather it is its inner didactic and moral qualities that may be shaped differently. The main point to stress is that the utterances are short and concise; lexical understanding is so subtle and associative that interest in the story's progression and solution is maintained right through to the end. The storyteller uses his imagination and talent to keep his listeners enthralled. Hence his language is close to "poetic fancy," *nduri.*[14] There is always a point to each particular story that highlights didactic, moral or behavioural ideas. Finally, the manner in which a *rungano* is delivered depends solely on the personality of the particular narrator. One may choose a

---

13. G.P. Kahari, "Tradition and Innovation in Shona Literature," *Zambezia* 2.2 (1972): 48.

14. See *Standard Shona Dictionary,* compiled by Michael Hannan (Harare: Literature Bureau, 1981). Under the noun *nduri* this reference is given: *Anotaura zvinofadza nokuti ane nduri*—"he talks pleasingly because he indulges his poetic fancy."

dramatic approach through gesture and of voice, another may intro-
duce the story/song in a more neutral—even monotonous—manner.
Whatever method is used, the tonal and rhythmic patterns of the
language are strictly adhered to.

One of the shortest *ngano* I have come across in Zimbabwe is a
story about the secretary bird and its imagined likeness to certain
women in the local environment. It carries the title *Pim'chinanga*. In
its most concentrated form it includes four short sentences—all
replied with the interjection *dzepfunde*. After the story has been told
the leader invites the participants to join in the singing, in which
humorous comments are made, for instance, about the similarities
between the animal and the human world. A chief's wife must be
respected, but at the same time you may dare a few comments about
her age and staggering walk, without commenting directly on her
personality.

Rungano "Pim'chinanga"

Storyteller	Response
Vamwe vakomana vakange vachifudza	
mombe mubani	*dzepfunde!*
Vakaona hwata yakange ichitsvaka hwiza	*dzepfunde!*
Vakarikidzwa nekufamba kwayo	*dzepfunde!*
Vakafunga kuti vaiimbire rumbo vachiiti	*dzepfunde!*
A number of boys were looking after cattle on a vlei	Hear!
They saw a secretary bird that was looking for locusts	Hear!
They were amused by the way it walked	Hear!
They planned to sing a song for it and said	Hear!

Muvambi (Leader)	*Vabvumiri* (Response)
Pim'chinanga, pim'chinanga	*Rire, rire m'chinanga*
(turn round and stare)	(look, look and stare)
Pim'chinanga, pim'chinanga	*Rire, rire m'chinanga*
Takaona hwata ichifamba	*Dzutarire m'chinanga*
(We saw a secretary bird walking)	(stop and look and stare)
Tikati taona mukaranga	*Dzutarire m'chinanga*
(We thought we had seen the Queen =	
the chief's wife; lit. an old Karanga	
[Shona] woman)	

The Shona song "Pim chinanga"

Application—an attempt at an analysis

Organised and publicly performed drama is not a common feature within the tradition of the Shona. Yet highly dramatic forms exist and appear spontaneously in daily life in certain situations. One such occasion, according to P. Matsikenyiri and T. C. Chawasarira,[15] is that of the threshing of grains at harvesting times of the year. There are numerous other occasions such as *bira* (in honour of ancestors) ceremonies, children's games, funerals etc. Thus the musical plays, music dramas, and the community theatre[16] have been introduced from the outside but they are all influenced by indigenous concepts of thinking. Interest in western drama and theatre was considerable among the Black population, even during the time of the white minority regime. The initiatives taken by churches and private theatre companies in the early 1960s may have had a role to play in expanding the drama.

---

15. Personal and verbal communication during interviews and other musical occasions.

16. See i.e. Lyrysa Smith, "Spotlight on community theatre," *Africa Calls*, no. 181, September/October 1990, Harare, 33–37 for a general review of community theatre. For an analytical study of theatre activities i Zimbabwe, community theatre included, see Preben Kaarsholm, "Mental Colonisation or Catharsis? Theatre, Democracy and Cultural Struggle from Rhodesia to Zimbabwe," *Journal of Southern African Studies* 16.2 (1990): 247–75.

The musical plays analysed in this context are widely known in Zimbabwe and produced locally in more or less the same way during certain times of the ecclesiastical calendar, particularly during Easter. Normally the same worked-out schedule of songs and drama is not applied, but the idea that it first and foremost serves a *functional* aspect is maintained, which is to make the biblical message more penetrating via poetry, drama, and song. As I indicated at the beginning of the chapter, such musical plays may have had a short life, but the actual *concept* they include continues to be used.

As mentioned earlier, the church drama *"Mazuva ekupedzisa"* composed by A.D. Maraire contains the Passion Story in which the biblical message has been re-dressed in poetical form and then set to music for the purpose of being performed. The story is divided into eight different scenes, each emphasizing important incidents pertaining to *"Via dolorosa"—The Road of Suffering.* It is mainly held together by a neutral narrator (*sarungano*). He brings the action forward almost in the same way as a narrator of a *rungano* would do, the only difference being that the narration is sung throughout the drama. The parts of Jesus, Peter, Mary, Judas the traitor, Pilate, and Mary Magdalene are sung. However, there are no solo performances; they are all accompanied by a choir. One could say that the choir acts according to three main principles. First, it represents the collective responses as in the structure of a *rungano* . Secondly, it achieves a more direct dramatic force as when individual actors sing their lines. Thirdly, it adopts a role of its own when it delivers messages from an outraged or deeply sorrowful crowd. It is apparent that the *ngano* is operating.

Apart from such general observations the subtitle of the drama also illustrates its relationship to the Shona *ngano* tradition as the term *mutambo* is used. The complete subtitle of the LP record reads: *Mutambo wekufa nekumuka kwaJesu wakanyoriwa sendwiyo muchiShona na Abraham Maraire.*[17] A direct translation would read: "The dramatic presentation of the death and resurrection of Jesus written in Shona by Abraham Maraire." According to Hannan the term *mutambo* stands for game, dramatic presentation, entertainment, and dance.[18] H. von Sicard notes that a verbal and common description of

---

17. *"Mazuva ekupedizisa"*; *Umbowo Records,* Church Music Service, P.B. 636 E, Salisbury, Rhodesia.
18. Hannan, *Standard Shona Dictionary.*

ngano may read: *Mutambo wokuita ngano navakuru* namai—("Telling of tales with mother and grown-ups") [my translation].[19]

Vocal Shona music has three parts. There is the leading part called *mushauri* (the one who leads; from *kushaura*—to lead), or *muvambi* (the one who begins; from *kuvamba*—to begin, or to start). The responsive character is either represented by the term *vatsinhiri* (those that follow; from *kutsinhira*—to add, to follow), or *vabvumiri* (those who are permitted; from *kubvumira*—to permit). Finally, as a fundamental "merger" of the two intertwining musical lines created by *mushauri* and *vatsinhiri,* there is always the *maho'nera* (*mahonyera*) bottom line; a vocal part which could be described in this context as a bass part. The literal meaning of the term is "sound of distant voices; humming."[20]

All songs in the Passion play by Maraire are based on the above musical structure that produces a harmonic experience of three to five vocal parts. This is because the *vatsinhiri* may hold more than one voice part. The aural perception is termed *tsinhirano.*[21]

In its most simple and direct form the structure of a song may appear as in the opening narrative of scene II. The complete song consists of nine stanzas of which three belong to the narrator; the latter is transcribed below. The narrator's presentation is neutral, reflecting the concept of a spoken *rungano*. The remaining six stanzas contain a dialogue between Jesus and Peter; thus they become more active and personal in opposition to the impersonal pattern of narration. However, the active response by the choir always appears at the end of each line: a sung interjection with the same function as the *dze-pfunde* interjection in a spoken *rungano*. This "collective" response does not suggest any specific meaning. On the contrary, it holds the same concept as the ambiguous meaning of *dzepfunde* and is expressed through vocables. In this context the response consists of the non-sensical words *i-ye, ye, ye*. Furthermore, all responding voice parts are to be comprehended as belonging to the *maho'nera*: the bottom line. Hence, it is experienced musically as a sonic background and perceived mentally as a more or less complete tonality veil to which the leader's line belongs.

---

19. H. von Sicard, "Karangamärchen," *Studia Ethnographica Upsaliensia* 23 (1965): xvi.
20. *Standard Shona Dictionary.*
21. *Ibid.*

Jesu wanga akagara	As Jesus was sitting
Nevadzidzi vake vese.	With all his disciples.
Vanga vava kuda kudya	They were about to eat
Chidyo chitsvene chekuguma.	The last supper.
Waiziva ngekufa kwake	He knew all about his death
Asi wanga asikatyiba.	But was not afraid.
Waiziva wakabva kuna Baba	He knew he came from his Father
Ndizvo wanga achienda	He would return to his Father.
kuna Baba.	
Wakasimuka, wakasimuka.	He stood up, he stood up.
Wakatora jira nemvura.	He took a towel and water.
Akavamba kugeza makumbo	He went to all his disciples
Evadzidzi vake vese.	And washed their feet.

The narration is brought forward through a medium that could be described as "sung speech rhythm." It is tempting at this point to use the term recitation in order to describe the narrator's "song." However, in doing so attention is drawn to the associations of free rhythm, which would be misleading in this context. Although the verse lines vary in length between eight to thirteen syllables, they are still sung in strict rhythm and seemingly experienced as groups of added blocks of two or three syllables. Thus the time-space of each line varies so that no metric division can be applied. Yet the response from the choir appears correct as seen against the narrator's asymmetric rhythmic flow. The result is a metric response based on three

times a 3-added unit. ⁞ ♩·⁞ . For this reason the time signature in the

musical transcription is noted as "additive quaver pulses" ⁞ ᶜ ⁞
and is to be understood as groups of two or three quavers.

The Shona drama song "Jesu wangu akagara"

The melodic line is extremely simple in structure, consisting only of a minor third in which the lower note holds the resting—hence the tonal—centre. This is apparently done only to emphasize the tonal structure of the phrases, i.e. the two basic spoken inflections in the Shona language.[22] The response by the choir starts from the lower pitch of the leader's line, only to fall another fourth down to a tonal centre as experienced by the first part of the response. The bottom

---

22. Derek Fivaz and Jeanette Ratzlaff, *Shona Language Lessons* (Bulawayo: Rhodesian Christian Press, 1969) 2.

part however takes this centre as its point of departure in order to arrive at a tonal centre yet another fifth down. The graphic illustration
below thus indicates three tonal areas which encompass a full octave
plus a minor third. This complete tonality area serves as a basic point
of departure for other songs in the drama of greater melodic and
harmonic structures.

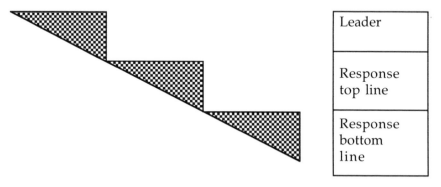

| Leader |
| Response top line |
| Response bottom line |

Interpreted into a musical score the graph above would be perceived
as follows:

Initial tonal area

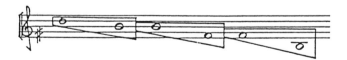

Moving along to scene III of the drama we enter the garden of
Gethsemane where, among other incidents, Jesus pours out his dis-
tress to his Father asking for redemption but yet confiding in the ab-
solute power of God; "not my will but Thine." There is also a narrator's part to move the story forward. This is immediately followed by
an anguished monologue by Jesus. Looking at the text and musical
scores below—or listening to a recorded version of this particular
song—it might be tempting to conclude that we have left the structure of a *rungano*. The song is now laid out metrically and there is a
continuous accompaniment in the lower sung parts. The interjections
by a participating collective group seem to have disappeared together with a *sung speech rhythm* in the leaders' voice as the melodies

are now much more prominent and definite. However, this is not the case. The composer still submits to the concepts of a traditional story, but he has expanded its form. The interjections have been made continuous to induce a feeling of deepened drama. Secondly, an increased intensity is achieved by the use of vocables that traditionally are associated with anguish and sorrow. The syllables *i-ri-ye wo-ye* often suggest crying, especially when used in a song in which the rhythm is slow.[23] And finally, the melodic lines of the narrator and Jesus follow the tonal qualities of spoken Shona, although being autonomous melodies.

Sarungano:

Apo Jesu anga ari kumirira kufa kwake,	While Jesus was awaiting his death
Wakakwira mugomo.	He went up on the mountain
Vadzidzi vake vese wakavasiya pasi	All his disciples were left below
Akakwira mugomo ega	He climbed the mountain alone.
Munamato wake ari imwo mugomo	While praying on the mountain
Kwenguva huru, wachiiti:	Praying for a long time, he said:

Jesus:

Baba wangu, regai uyu mukombe	My Father, let this cup
Upfuure, kwandiri; upfuure kwandiri.	Let it pass from me, pass from me
Baba wangu, haiwa sezvondinoda	My Father, not as I want
Asi sezvomunoda, itai Baba.	But as you want, let it be done, Father.

Comparing the poetic structure of the two poems so far dealt with, we find that the first poem in scene II contains four-line stanzas of approximately the same length throughout. Yet the musical solution of those stanzas has been arrived at through the use of additional rhythmic units based on language rhythm and structure, to which a more symmetrical and metric response has been added. In the latter case the poetic structure is built on two-lined stanzas. As for the narrator's part, each first line of all the three stanzas is longer as com-

---

23. Personal communication with P. Matsikenyiri and T.C. Chawasarira, in addition to statements made by numerous other Shona musicians.

pared to each second line. This effect has been reached by the introduction of additional information about the actions taken, combined
with subtle and associative implications, whereas each second line
contains a simpler, and more straightforward statement. In spite of
this verbal expansion and increased complexity, the musical structure adopts the form of an ostinato metre based on an isorhythmic
pattern which is repeated four times. This occurs in the lower accompanying sung parts as well as in the leader's melodic and isorhythmic phrase.

The Shona song "Apo Jesu anga"

The composer uses the tonal centres of the previous song as points of departure for an extention of the tonal area, while keeping to the spoken framework. In this way a faster learning of new musical phrases is made possible . Due to the extended use of the initial tonal centre and the memorization of the words, the melodic lines are kept alive. The shaping of formulæ for melodic units derives from the tonal centres. In addition, the isorhythmic structure of each melodic line enhances the learning process.

Extended tonal area

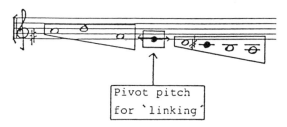

Isorhythmic structure

Muvambi
(Leader)

Vabvumiri
(Response)

In the first part of the song (above) there is no direct conflict of metre between the different sung parts. The leader and the respondents co-operate in the musical and narrative progression. However, when Jesus enters the scene, a dramatic change takes place in the balancing of the leading part and the two-part ostinato. The changes occur in the melodic line presented by the main actor Jesus, in the tonal area and in the rhythmic structure. Whereas the tonal emphasis has previously been on the pitches a, b, f sharp, d, and with the final resting on low a, the ambitus of the melodic line is now extended in an upward direction. The emphasis of important pitches seems to circle around the pitches d and a, and a stress on the pivot area, i.e. the pitches e and b through the addition of the falling triad b, g, and d before the note e.

The Shona song "Baba wangu"

The conflicting metric rhythms create polyrhythms and are used to stress the conflict in the actual scene.

Conflicting isorhythmic structure

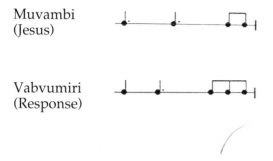

Muvambi
(Jesus)

Vabvumiri
(Response)

Mweya waMwari (The Spirit of God) by J. Mushuku, J. Nduna and
P. Matsikenyiri

The liberation war in Zimbabwe escalated and intensified during the
1970s and increased the suffering that affected large parts of both the
rural and urban population. At this time there was a growing desire
within voluntary and ecumenical church organisations that teaching
should employ more advanced illustrations to better the unjust political and economic life of the country.[24] Therefore, towards the end of
1977, ideas of a new church music drama emerged. By early 1978 two
leading students and composers at Kwanongoma College of Music in
Bulawayo, J. Mushuku and J. Nduna, together with one of the most
outstanding composers of the country, P. Matsikenyiri from Mutam-
bara in eastern Zimbabwe, were joined by staff and students at the
College to work for a month on the ideas of a church music drama
called *Mweya waMwari* ("The Spirit of God") [see footnote 7]. Once
completed, it was performed in some of the city churches on three
different occasions during the Holy Week. Shortly afterwards the
play was performed several times by the College in both Sweden and
Finland during a four-week concert tour supported by the Church of
Sweden Mission and some Lutheran church organisations in
Germany and Finland.

---

24. See "We are His Creation," presented by the Ecumenical Arts Association of
Zimbabwe, Umtali, 1979.

As mentioned earlier, the drama is built on several biblical stories that illustrate both harmonious and disharmonious relationships between God and Man. These two disparate images project the principal themes of the play, the concept of order as opposed to the concept of chaos. The supreme and omnipotent *Mwari* (God) stands for order and *Munhu* (man), through his continual desire to break his relationship with the Supreme, disrupts the harmony of creation so that chaos, similar to the initial chaos before creation, is brought back into the life of humanity.

> As the waves of the sea rise and fall—so also with human life. In the very timeless beginning there was complete chaos—nothingness. Yet, God's omnipotence ruled supreme—and He acted. The encompassing wave of Creation emerged and chaos was changed into order. Man—the reflection of God himself—became the climax of life and creation. And the Spirit of God was with Man—and in Man. ...
>
> The Bible tells us the story—but it has eternal implications. Whenever Man rejects the Spirit of God within him the result is chaos—whenever he accepts and follows the Spirit of God there is deliverance and liberation. Man's disobedience against creation leads to death—to oppression; but to listen and follow the Spirit of God brings liberation from destruction and chaos—and Man again lives in God's Love—and God's Love lives in Man.
>
> Thus, this musical drama is like waves on the sea, illustrating Man's desire for liberation in a whole and true sense.[25]

The story's four dramatic scenes illustrating well-known biblical incidents are held together by the dichotomy expressed in God's longing for harmony and order, and the constant activities of man which disrupt such harmony. Emphasis is placed on the mediating instrument of the supernatural power and humanity, i.e. *Mweya* (the spirit). The short initial theme song, repeated throughout the drama in different musical guises, includes a direct quotation from Genesis 1:2, *Mweya waMwari waigara/pamsoro pemvura* ("The Spirit of God hovered/over the waters").[26] The formal structure is laid out similar to a Shona proverb, i.e. in a bipartite form.

The first scene illustrates God's initial action: chaos is turned into order by the creation of nature into which man and woman are ultimately introduced. Darkness is changed into light and in this light

---

25. Accompanying textsheet inside record folder of the LP record "Vibrant Zimbabwe," *PROP 7808*, 1979.
26. The complete text of the drama "Mweya waMwari" is found on the accompanying textsheet. See note 25 above.

man takes possession of nature in the image of his Creator. Driven by selfish purposes, however, humanity runs into conflict with God. This is represented in the play by short biblical incidents. The mediating instrument *Mweya* is discarded, which results in death, war and oppression exemplified by the enmity of Cain and Abel; the enslaved period in Egypt; the years of wandering in the desert; and the disruptive life in the promised land before the advent of Jesus Christ. The third scene describes the birth of Christ, his teaching and his death on the cross. With his coming into the world, peace and salvation are anticipated through the declarations of the prophet Isiah. Conflicts continue, however, culminating in the ultimate chaos with the crucifixion of *Mwana waMwari* (the Son of God). In the concluding and fourth scene, through the resurrection of Christ, *Mweya* (the Spirit) once again becomes instrumental in the life of mankind. The drama thus ends in the hopeful belief expressed by the chorus of Matsikenyiri's song to the Holy Spirit:

> *Mweya Mutsvene Baba, Mweya, Mweya*
> (The Holy Spirit, Father, Spirit, Spirit)
> *Mweya Mutsvene Baba, chisungo chedu.*
> (The Holy Spirit, Father, unites us all)

The overall structure of the drama discards the idea of a *sarungano* (narrator) unlike the case of *Mazuva ekupedzisa* where the storyteller is constantly present. It is only at the beginning of the play that a single voice is briefly heard reciting the opening verses of Genesis over the tumultuous and chaotic sounds preceding the initial creation activities by *Musiki* (the creator). Instead narration becomes a natural collective concept in the actual presentation of all songs. Although it is possible to superimpose the general structure of a *rungano* (traditional story) onto the drama, the particular ingredients of a single storyteller and a collective response group are missing. The choir is used as an active collective group in the action of the drama, as well as a commentator, as the songs are dramatized. Yet, the format is based on traditional ideas. Most of the songs pursue patterns similar to traditional oral poetry, either spoken, intoned, or sung.[27] Biblical stories have been transformed into idiomatic Shona constructions through the use of poetry, which is a common procedure for most traditional poetry in southern Africa. The three composers and poets have made use of their innate talents: *Vanotaura*

---

27. Fortune, "Shona Traditional Poetry," *Zambezia* 2.1 (1971): 42.

zvinofadza nokuti vane nduri or "they talk pleasingly because they in-
dulge their poetic fancy." According to Fortune, Shona poetry essentially consists of

> ... the aesthetic necessity of form which gives unity and satisfactory complete-
> ness to a poem and to its constituent parts. Imagery with repetition,...combine
> to make poetry more evocative, more emotive and more memorable than other
> forms of speech and issue in a greater richness and concentration of language.[28]

Functional aspects

Bearing such literary forms in mind, it is necessary to comment
briefly on the socio-political aspects of the two music dramas discussed here at the time of their appearance. From 1964 when the
guerilla group called the "Crocodile Gang" made its first incursion
into the country then called Rhodesia, the liberation war gathered
new impetus and gradually escalated. The *Chimurenga II* had com-
menced in earnest.[29] Thereafter the determination to liberate the
country from the white minory rule became more intense. There is
no need here to retrace all political, military, and guerilla developments. Yet it is necessary to outline briefly the implicit characteristics
of the term *chimurenga* so that a workable hypothesis may be formulated on the functional implications of the two dramas.

Chimurenga has come to mean *liberation*. Hence the expression
rwiyo ngezva chimurenga—"songs about liberation." According to
Hannan,[30] it may either denote "riot" or "fighting in which everyone
joins." The historic importance of the term can be traced back to the
time when the Black population revolted against white colonialism
and dominion in the 1890s. Those events are referred to as
Chimurenga I. However, the term may also have wider religious implications relating to Shona traditional religion, as it seems to be
derived from the word *Murenga* which is a substitute for *Mwari*,
God or Supreme Being. At the same time *murenga* also means a war-
like spirit. Thus there are implicit religious concepts involved when
the Shona use the term *chimurenga* in the sense of liberation.

---

28. Fortune 42. See also A.T. Cope, *Izibongo: Zulu Praise Poems* (Oxford: Clarendon
Press, 1968).
29. Michael Raeburn, *Black Fire! Accounts of the Guerilla War in Zimbabwe* (Gwelo
[Gweru]: Mambo Press, 1979) 1.
30. *Standard Shona Dictionary.*

During the entire struggle for freedom in Zimbabwe, liberation songs were continuously used for the purpose of political awareness. Quite naturally the white minority regime banned songs with such a content. However, the ZANLA and ZIPRA guerila groups established their own choirs with the effect that liberation songs were broadcast on the radio from frontline states as well as performed both in guerila camps outside the country, and inside the country at nightly and secret meetings with the local population. Such meetings came to be called *pungwe*. The political messages of the liberation songs were usually clear. No ambiguities were necessary to deceive the enemy.

Apart from the political songs learnt and memorized at nightly and secret gatherings, another kind of liberation song emerged inside the country. These, however, had to be structured in a manner deceptive to the minority regime. Hence, the texts were built on idiomatic Shona, on proverbs, convoluted syntax, and deliberate ambiguities which became "veritable political landmines on which the white regime of the day sat with ignorant equanimity."[31] The melodies were either adaptations of already well-known songs— quite often Christian melodies of western origin—or new melodies which emerged as the text was being composed. Little is known about these songs. The objective of these songs was to make the oppressed people conscious of their situation.

We need to stress the great importance of the inside initiatives in the liberation process. The inside activities analysed in Pongweni's book centre mainly on popular music performers whom he refers to as the "home artists."[32] Local pop stars such as T. Mapfumo and O. Mutukudzve—internationally recognized and hailed—certainly played an important role in the political process—roles they have continued to shoulder even during the present post-independence period. It is, however, necessary to classify further the songs performed inside the country. To the category of "home artists" also belonged a large number of lesser-known performers who were actively involved in the struggle for political awareness. They worked on a much smaller scale in their local environments. I am particularly referring to the voluntary activities organized by local Christian communities in which talented people made use of their skills in

---

31. Alec J.C. Pongweni, Preface, *Songs That Won the Liberation War* (Harare: College Press, 1982).
32. *Ibid.* 1.

composing Christian songs for use in church services and at rallies. Such activities were already spearheaded in the 1950s by a few de- nominations.[33] With the establishment of the _Ecumenical Arts Association_ in Bulawayo in 1968 the aim of associating Christian teaching with the demands of the social environment became more prominent.[34] Hence we can justifiably speak about _chimurenga_ songs within a Christian environment. Unfortunately, the attempts of the Christian movements to advance this view have been veiled in favour of the aspirations of the liberation forces and popular secular activities. In addition it is important to stress that the "home artists" in Pongweni's study made extensive use of Christian, and/or tradi- tional, religious concepts in their songs.

It is within this realm that the two dramas should be perceived. There is no doubt that the message of the second drama, _Mweya waMwari_, reinterprets biblical teaching, highlighting conflict-torn social life in the Zimbabwe of the 1970s. The dichotomies of order versus disorder, harmony versus disharmony, peace versus war and conflict were all analogous to what the general population experi- enced during the liberation struggle. The action of Cain slaying Abel at the beginning of the drama alludes to the history of Zimbabwe at the end of the last century when the foundations of white supremacy were established. Hence, the short, but dramatic, wailing and proverb-like sentence in the middle of the no. 6 war song:

Ndooneswa nhamo; Munyika yandakazvarirwa.
(We are suffering; In our land of birth)

Numerous examples could be given of such analogies. Suffice it to mention in this context song no. 7b which deals with the promise of deliverance from slavery in Egypt. The song was composed by J. Nduna to the accompaniment of the traditional and popular Shona instrument, the _mbira_. The full text of the song reads:

---

33. O.E. Axelsson, "Historical Notes on Neo-African Church Music," _Zambezia_ 3.2 (1974): 89–102.
34. "We are His Creation," presented by the Ecumenical Arts Association, Umtali, 1979.

Mwana washe muranda kumwe;	The son of the chief
Iri ishoko	is servant in foreign land;
rakarehwa noungwaru	wisely this message
Benzi iti ziro	was delivered.
ugokudzwa somungwaru.	Remain quiet
Tova chipfuva chako	and be wise.
nedova nhaka.	Patience
	is required.
Panguwa yedu	We are still
ino tichiri mupfumvu.	in bondage.
Ngatiregei	Let us not have
kurasa miromo yedu;	loose talk;
Faro akatinzwa	if Pharaoh
tichigungura kudai.	hears us talking
Haangakoni	he will destroy
kupedza upenyu hwedu.	our lives.
Uyai vanhu vose,	Come all people,
titivere Moses wedu;	and follow Moses;
Dakara tasvika	until we reach
kunyika yeKenani.	the land of Canaan.
Faro achasara	Pharaoh will remain
achichema zvikuru;	worried;
kusuwa nhapwa dzake	thinking about all his slaves
dzaaivimba nadzo.	whom he used to have.

The first line of the song is a direct quotation from a Shona proverb. Its original meaning according to Hamutyinei and Plangger is that "Whatever your status in life among your own people, you cannot expect to be treated accordingly when you are away from home. Among strangers, you are just a passer-by."[35] In this song, however, the proverb seems to suggest a wider and more subtle interpretation. In this context *Mwana washe* (the chief's son) refers to all Black people who have received their birthright to their country through their ancestors. This birthright was violated by the colonialists and the chief's son, the entire Black population, was forced to become a mere servant. Hence the proverb is a guideline for how further action could be instigated to retrieve this birthright. Then it also becomes evident that Pharaoh represents the white minority regime while Moses represents the leaders of the two liberation movements ZANU

---

35. *Tsumo—Shumo; Shona Proverbial Lore and Wisdom,* 312.

and ZAPU. So here we have a political programme in a Christian literary framework.

This chapter on Christian poetry and music drama in Zimbabwe demonstrates then that much of contemporary Black church music in Zimbabwe follows indigenous patterns.

The "Electronic Church" in a Zimbabwean Communication Environment

Hilde Arntsen and Knut Lundby

Africa and particularly African traditional religions have long held a grip on both European missionaries and researchers. To date, the popular notions of the African multiple layers of traditions and beliefs continue to hold the fascination of those coming from the northern hemisphere. The great commission of the followers of the Christian faith, the spreading of the Word, has not only carried missionaries to the African continent in large numbers, it is still continuing to have a bearing on people and evangelists from the "first world." The African scene is thus no longer merely populated by missionaries in the traditional sense; the missionaries or evangelists of today are to an increasing degree employing the mass media. The use of the mass media as tools for spreading Christianity may even entail that the evangelists do not have to be physically present in the sense the missionaries used to be. Trans World Radio can serve as one example of how a radio network has been developed with a view of spreading the Gospel by means of short wave radio.[1] The use of television for religious purposes is a phenomenon of a more recent date, but nevertheless one claimed to be more powerful by senders and critics alike. As the television evangelist Pat Robertson has claimed: "We're influencing the nations through Christian broadcasting."[2]

To date, not much media research has been carried out on religious television broadcasting outside of the United States, and particularly not in an African context. It is in our view now appropriate critically to investigate religious broadcasting as a world-wide phenomenon. In addition to studying the international context of such a phenomenon, it is of particular importance to include the audiences' reactions to such programming. The presence of international media

---

1. Fortner, 1990: 307–28.

2. Harrell, 1987.

products around the world cannot tell us anything about its impact, or how the audiences understand and make use of the contents.[3]

It has been argued that the media are American,[4] indicating that the formats and genres which influence the media throughout the world are based on the standards set by the commercial mass media in the United States. The structures behind the international media or the homogenising of the media content have thus often been the focus of study. The focus in terms of religious media has also been on the American scene. The "return of the powerful viewer" in international media research triggered a number of studies of audience reactions. But to the best of our knowledge, the scope has only to a limited degree been utilised on a global scale.[5] We have attempted to rectify this by beginning to investigate the advent and expansion of religious broadcasting to Zimbabwe and audience reactions to this phenomenon. One may later begin to address the question whether this is cultural domination to be equated with the missionaries' efforts to spread the Bible, and thereby European and American culture.

The missionaries' task was to make people accept the Bible and its teachings. The development aid workers' task of today can likewise be regarded as making people accept the ways and means of the development agency, in most cases a western agency ruled by western European or American values. The development aid organisations do seldom, however, admit that they may be "missionaries" in the true sense of the word.[6] What, then, is then the case with modern mass media?

Despite technically advanced media, the transmission of the message is still to a considerable degree one-way both in technical and in structural terms. This can be regarded as a classic example of cultural imperialism, or in this context, media imperialism. Proponents of the imperialism thesis may argue that the mere presence of powerful international media structures is a trait of media imperialism. Cultural imperialism, as the more holistic term of the two, may refer to the dependence and dominance relationships of uneven international

---

3. See for instance Gentikow, 1989.

4. Tunstall, 1977.

5. One notable exception to this is Liebes & Katz, 1990.

6. Tvedt, 1990: 30–36.

power dimensions.[7] Boyd-Barrett defines media imperialism as follows:

> The process whereby the ownership, structure, distribution or content of the media in any one country are singly or together subject to substantial external pressures from the media interests of any other country or countries without proportionate reciprocation of influence by the country so affected.[8]

Regardless of how the imperialism term is being viewed today, it does have its shortcomings. While most theories have emphasised the structural imbalances behind international media, ownership and control of the media, or the origin of the media content,[9] we would like to argue that including the audiences' own readings of the available media content may alter the pessimistic picture somewhat.

The "Electronic Church" from the United States to Zimbabwe

Religious broadcasting, often referred to as the "electronic church," is a good example of uneven transnational media networks which are now attempting to transgress the world.[10] The phenomenon of the "electronic church" grew out of fundamentalist and conservative religious movements in the United States, but the term itself was not coined until 1979 in an era of technological optimism to denote what was then perceived as a religious collectivity to be created by the electronic media.[11] Religious television broadcasting in the United States was transformed with the advent of the "electronic churches." From what had been mere television transmittal of public meetings, religious broadcasts were created specifically for television. In many respects the genres and formats of commercial television were employed in religious television as well.[12] Spreading this outside of the United States may thus not only propagate an American style kind of religion, it may also be closely linked to the expansion of American cultures, American media formats and perhaps the "American

---

7. See, for instance, Murdock & Golding, 1977.

8. Boyd-Barrett, 1977: 117.

9. See, for instance, Tunstall, 1977, or Lee, 1980.

10. Bruce, 1990.

11. Frankl, 1987.

12. Hoover, 1988.

Dream." What Quentin Schultze has termed the "mythos of the electronic church,"[13] the uncritical technological optimism that links the electronic media with the providential mission to preach the gospel around the world, seems to be the modern version of the missionaries activities.

The programmes of one such "electronic church" are broadcast on television in Zimbabwe (ZBC TV1), *The 700 Club*, from the American televangelist and former presidential candidate, Marion G. "Pat" Robertson.[14] *The 700 Club* is a re-edited so-called "international" version of Pat Robertson's *700 Club* which is aired on the Christian Broadcasting Network (CBN) in the United States. *The 700 Club* was chosen as the object of study both because it is shown in Zimbabwe[15] and because it has been regarded as the quintessential example of the "electronic church" genre:[16] making use of the familiar formats of American commercial television, it can for instance be seen as a religious talk show or a religious news cast.

Religion and mass communication

Communication can be conceptualised through its aspect of community, i.e. shared rituals and symbols. The linear model of communication, the one-way transmission of messages from one or a few senders to many receivers continues to be a misleading interpretation. But this nevertheless continues to be the prevailing mode of mass communication, where the feedback from the audience to the sender is virtually non-existent, or if existing, is funneled through other channels. Religion as communication, and religion as the content of communication, can only be understood by means of ritual and symbolic communication, as Michael Bourdillon maintains in his sociology of religion in an African context.[17] Religion must be understood on the basis of the local context or the local *communication envi-*

---

13. Schultze, 1987.

14. Pat Robertson campaigned for presidential nomination for the Republican party in the United States in 1988.

15. *The 700 Club* is supplied to ZBC free of charge, and broadcast once a week, around noon Sundays. Manners Mvudura, Programme Procurement Officer, ZBC, Harare, 11 September 1991.

16. Hoover, 1988: 60.

17. Bourdillon, 1990.

ronment.[18] Religious communication by means of the mass media can therefore be regarded as a contradiction in terms, regardless of the attempts to create communication environments, as we shall attempt to demonstrate below.

Communication environment

Communication unfolds as the handling of symbols in a *communication environment* with certain social and material characteristics. We understand the communication environment as the social and material surroundings for the communicating person. A communication environment is created and maintained through the material infrastructure. It is also created through the meaningful human interaction and communication within and related to the material surroundings. A communication environment is thus a social material field of action.[19] A communication environment is defined through its social and material character, but a communication environment will always have a specific symbolic capacity.

Communication can be defined as "social interaction through messages,"[20] in other words that which constitutes an individual in her or his society. Inevitably, such human interaction must take place in time and space, and in certain material surroundings. The media are a part of this; as they are a part of the symbolic life or social community. We can moreover say that symbolic meaning is attached to social life by means of the material carriers or vehicles. The meanings of a symbol are continuously determined through convention. A "symbol" is here defined as a culturally conditioned sign. As Durkheim demonstrated, even religion, the carrier of sacred symbolic meanings, is based in a social setting.[21] Uprooting a religious sign from one cultural context and attempting to transplant it into another will thus entail different meanings, something which has been more thoroughly discussed within the tradition of semiotics.

Durkheim's definition of religion is based on its rites, its community of the sacred, set apart from the profane:

---

18. Lundby, 1992.
19. Østerberg, 1990: 66–79.
20. Fiske, 1982:2.
21. Durkheim, 1968.

A religion is a unified system of beliefs and practices relative to sacred things, that is to say, things set apart and forbidden—beliefs and practices which unite into one single moral community called a Church, all those who adhere to them.[22]

Durkheim's theory of religion and society is applicable to Africa precisely because it emphasises the connection between the communication with the sacred and the communication within the social group.[23] The rites and the systems of beliefs which are carriers of the sacred must be repeated in order to maintain the religious community. A moral community then, according to Durkheim, is based in social interaction. A religious community must therefore be a social community. Religiosity is based in social relationships. Symbols are thus continuously reformulated, and their interpretation takes place through their inclusion in the moral community. This can, for instance, be seen in Zimbabwe's independent churches, which voice a *Quest for Belonging*.[24]

The ambiguity of the media

The communication environment can be studied at different levels, for instance a particular village or city, or rather parts of those localities based upon gender, social class, ethnicity, or tribe. A communication environment is as we have seen based on interaction and identification between the people and their community. The physical environment is a part of the communication environment through determining the conditions for symbolic exchange. The material structures are part of the communication environment because they are human-made, cultural products. More important, however, is the fact that the *media* utilised in the communication are themselves part of the communication environment in question.

Let us take an example: a church is then at the same time both a physical environment surrounding the congregation assembled for worship, and a symbolic environment encompassing the congregation, its rites and communication. The communication will invariably

---

22. Durkheim, 1968: 47.
23. Bourdillon, 1990: 6–34.
24. Daneel, 1987.

have to take place within the physical boundaries of the building or within the immediate vicinity of the tree under the which the congregation assembles. This particular communication environment may in turn be a part of a larger communication environment, or the members of the congregation may belong to various localities or communication environments.

There is an ambiguity in the carriers or vehicles used in communication. They are carriers of symbols, but at the same time they are symbols themselves. In the same vein, we can see that culture is formed by the human beings within it, while at the same time culture forms those very same people.[25] This constructivism is thus also a fact of communication. Language and media render the symbolic exchange within the communication environment possible. As Raymond Williams has pointed out, television as a medium is both technology and cultural form.[26] This ambiguity of the symbolic carriers increases as the use of the technical media intensifies. Impulses from the outside are then fed into the communication environment by the means of the technical media. For instance, concepts introduced by *The 700 Club* may at first seem remote, even unintelligible or irrelevant to the viewers, but television will, at least according to Dahlgren,[27] alter what is new, unintelligible or exotic into items which become a part of our cultural terms of reference.

Communication by means of technical media may lead to increased globalisation,[28] which may result in the development of transnational networks of symbols.[29] One question, then, is whether these transnational networks constitute communication environments. New technologies have facilitated a transnational material structure, to date primarily in urban settings, but there must also be a social structure within the material framework. Communication linked to social interaction must take place on a regular basis. Only then can a communication environment be established.

---

25. See, for instance, Dahlgren, 1990: 63.
26. Williams, 1975.
27. Dahlgren, 1990: 77.
28. Robertson, 1990; Giddens, 1989, ch. 16.
29. Featherstone, 1990.

Tradition and modernity

Secularisation has become a trait of modern society. This is the case for Zimbabwean society as well. But, maintains Bourdillon, "perhaps instead of thinking in terms of the decline of the sacred, we should be looking for changes in what is sacred."[30] He does not accept the notion that the scientifically based rationality of the western modernity is superior. The traditional religiosity has its own rationality, he maintains: "What is largely true is that in traditionally religious systems, knowledge is assumed to come largely from the past and wisdom to lie with elders, whereas in the scientific system, the past is constantly superseded and has no authority of its own."[31] In this manner, the "electronic church" can thus be said to constitute a break from tradition into modernity.

Sid Ahmed Nugdalla, who is writing from a Sudanese perspective, poses the opposition to the western duality-thinking of modernity *versus* traditionalism, in his article in the book *The African Experience: Making Broadcasting Useful* which deals with the development of radio and television in Africa in the 1980s.[32] Nugdalla sees modernity as "inseparable from traditionalism; and modernisation in culture, agriculture, or industry is nothing but the transformation of tradition." His point is that most African countries represent a combination of tribal societies and developing or modernising culture or cultures. There one can find a process of slow, ambivalent cultural change, rather than a complete shift from traditionalism to modernity.[33] We do not necessarily agree with him, as this may be too simplistic a view. But that view points precisely to these *tensions* in the processes of cultural change that need to be studied. Hence, we have to seek the arenas where the cultural changes are unfolding. One such arena is *The 700 Club* and its well-wrapped American television messages.

Generally speaking, the African continent meets us with a "predominantly traditional social structure."[34] Within this framework, or in more specific communication environments, we can find the

---

30. Bourdillon, 1990: 294–95.
31. Bourdillon, 1990: 226.
32. Nugdalla, 1986: 93.
33. Cfr. Melkote, 1991: 39–40.
34. Nugdalla, 1986: 93.

struggles with modern influences. For instance, the struggle between Islamisation and secularisation of the state or the conflict between modernity and tradition among university students, to mention but two examples. They are struggles on the symbolic definition of reality. They are struggles of how to represent values, norms, ideas, attitudes, and other components of culture. Such changes in a communication environment may be provoked by changes in processes as those of urbanisation and industrialisation. Changes in representations or images in the culture will on the other hand also feed back into the communication environment.

Time and space

The electronic media may transgress the barriers of time and space: the production of symbols may take place far away from where the symbol users are physically situated. The production may also take place without time delay, such as with live television transmissions, for instance the media events of royal weddings,[35] or a soccer match.[36] Such symbolic import may increase the symbolic complexity of the communication environment. This may for instance happen when *The 700 Club* makes use of typical symbols for the "American Dream," stressing the individuality of the being in society, or otherwise introduces symbols which otherwise would not have been present in the culture or the communication environment in question.

Although the symbolic surroundings are wide and fluctuating, communication as the handling of symbols *takes place* within a social material field of action restricted by time and space. The symbol users are at the same time symbol producers at their own level by means of their own interpretation of symbols. Everyone who is part of the social life thus participates in the social construction of reality.[37] The theory of the social construction of reality provides insight into the symbolic surroundings as part of the communication environment, and the dynamics between the two. Durkheim's notion of society as a reality in itself is here supplemented by a view of the active human being. Berger & Luckmann emphasised the point that we

---

35. See, for instance, Chaney, 1986.
36. Altheide & Snow, 1979.
37. Berger & Luckmann, 1971.

encounter society as an objective reality which we ourselves participate in constructing. This may inevitably always take place within
the realms of communication environments, as a social basis, to continue Berger & Luckmann's terminology. This furthermore points to
the applicability of religion as an object of study.

Religion thus provides a valid example of the social construction
of reality precisely as it provides the utmost basis for the symbolic
universe: The superstructure which ties together various "provinces
of meaning" and which thus constitutes society as a "symbolic total-
ity."[38] But, the question remains whether religion in the mass media
have strong enough support in communication environments created
around the audiences to provide a sound social basis or plausibility
structure. According to our interviewees, this was not the case with
The 700 Club in Zimbabwe.[39]

Cultural tensions

In a study of media use in Kenya, Minou Fuglesang[40] provides a
vivid illustration of the difference between the social material communication environment and its local symbolic universe. In Lamu,
Kenya, imported Indian films were actively used in the construction
of the audiences' symbolic universe, particularly among young
women. The fact that the films largely drew upon a Hindu symbolic
universe while the women were Muslim, was apparently of minor
importance to the women themselves. As Lamu is located on an is-
land off the coast of Kenya, it can easily be set apart as a separate
communication environment. The symbolic universe available within
this social material field of action is, however, more complex. The
Indian films are utilised in the tensions or negotiations between old
and new values and modes of being within the said communication
environment. It is worth noting, however, that such importing of
symbols does not automatically lead to immediate and direct influences. Through their reinterpretation of the symbolic material in the

---

38. Berger & Luckmann, 1971.

39. The interviews were conducted by H. Arntsen, with thanks to the kind assistance from our colleagues at the University of Zimbabwe, September, 1991.

40. Fuglesang, 1990.

films, the women demonstrated the resistance against foreign symbol products which is inherent in the communication environment.

Today, a large extent of the symbolic content which is at use in a certain communication environment has been produced in other cultures. The use of the technical media renders it possible to cross the boundaries of the communication environment thereby bringing in symbolic content from the outside. *Culture* is created and maintained through communication.[41] Any culture emerges as a symbolic system where the differences are brought out through the utilisation of symbolic power based on "symbolic capital"[42] in the processes tied to the production and use of these symbols.

The communication environment provides a *plausibility structure* or social base[43] for the symbols which people encounter in their respective cultures. A social basis for the symbolic reality is provided by the material and social structure in the said field of action and the social cultural processes that take place there. This may contribute to rendering the content of symbols and meaning credible for the participants in the communication environment, provided there is interplay between the two.

In the United States, attempts are made to create communication environments around the telecasts of the "electronic church" by means of parachurch activities such as mail services, local viewer groups, telephone counselling services, universities etc. But the case outside the United States may in several instances be far from these well-functioning networks. It is thus important to question whether it is at all possible to create a communication environment by transplanting symbolic material from an American "electronic church" in another cultural context, in this case Zimbabwe. Attempts are made to transfer this concept from the United States to the local society. We thus find attempt to combine the television message with other communicative forms and transferring the communication activities from one cultural context to another: the co-operating agency in Harare, which claims to be independent of CBN, is primarily a marriage counselling centre, offering counelling sessions and classes. Participants are solicited through the network of religious groups in

---

41. Lundby & Rønning, 1991.

42. Bourdieu, 1977: 171–83.

43. Berger & Luckmann, 1971, Berger, 1969.

Harare.[44] Although *The 700 Club* does not constitute a major part of the centre's activities, this is in our view an example of the combined communication strategies and an attempt to create a support environment for the television programme. It remains to be seen whether this is the case.

Unbalanced networks and The 700 Club

Power is inevitably always unequally distributed in terms of technologically mediated communication and interaction. The ones in control of the technical infrastructure do of course have a larger degree of influence than those who merely control their own attention to the message. Unless the receivers are actively decoding the message through the consumption and interpretation of symbols, no relations will be established, and hence no communication. The receivers are equipped with a number of filters such as selective attention, selective perception, filtering of the message through the immediate social environment and previous personal experience etc.[45]

People playing down the alleged harmful effects of foreign television content often argue that television is of minor importance in the third world as it is mostly a privilege of the urban rich.[46] In Zimbabwe, television viewing is unevenly distributed both socially and geographically; it is first and foremost an urban phenomenon.[47] Also, television viewing is unevenly distributed throughout the day, with the highest viewership figures in "prime time" between eight and nine p.m, when the news and "Dynasty" compete for the highest figures.[48] In our view it is too simplistic to dismiss the discussion of influence on grounds of technology.

---

44. Interview with one director of New Hope Centre, Harare, September 1991.

45. For a more thorough discussion of these processes, see, for instance, Waldahl, 1991.

46. Varis, 1974: 107.

47. Estimated number of working television sets in Zimbabwe: Low density areas: approximately 54,300 colour television sets, and 36,800 black and white sets, compared with 4,280 colour sets and 94,090 black and white sets in high density areas. The corresponding figures for rural areas are 110 colour sets and 8,700 black and white sets. Source: Value Survey 1990, Phobe Market Research, Harare.

48. Source: Value Survey 1990, Phobe Market Research, Harare.

The availability of communication technology also has another question. One of the most prominent features of *The 700 Club* concept is the offer for prayer counselling over the telephone. In the United States, telephone prayer counselling centres have been established around the country. The concluding scenes in the programme assert:

> "When you need to talk with someone who cares, call *The 700 Club* and talk with a friend, someone who will listen and someone who cares enough to pray with you. Pick up the phone and call *The 700 Club*. We're here when you need us," and further "When you need to talk to someone who cares, *The 700 Club* has telephone prayer counsellors standing by to answer your call. *The 700 Club* cares about you, so call or write their offices in your country today."[49]

It may be argued that *The 700 Club* attempts at building a social material field of action around the telecasts, by means of elements of the parachurch. It is thus a paradox that *The 700 Club* on ZBC only lists a contact address with a post office box in a Harare suburb. One of the main aspects of *The 700 Club* as an "electronic church," the quasi collectivity attempted through telephone contact with viewers, has thus been reduced to a mere mail response service.[50] As one of our respondents remarked, "we can't sort of pick up the phone and dial...."[51] "Being there" when people need them can hardly be said to be the case here, and thus hardly the existence of a communication environment.

The export of media content is one trait of media imperialism, be it within entertainment programming generally or *The 700 Club* specifically. When the bulk of a country's television content is produced outside the particular cultural sphere, or communication environment, or when foreign contents set the standard by which domestic productions are judged, this can be regarded as imperialism, according to Boyd-Barrett. Dealing with a religious programme genre which views itself as a church rather than just another television programme compels us, however, also to discuss the question beyond the imperialism parameter. It is in our view not possible for

---

49. *The 700 Club*, taped from ZBC at various times during 1991, © CBN 1990.

50. The follow-up in Zimbabwe is administered by personnel at the New Hope Centre, which also refers to itself as International 700 Club, Zimbabwe Ministry Centre. Although it claims to be financially independent of CBN, CBN supplies some publications material, and statistics of letters from the public are submitted to CBN regularly.

51. Interview with female students, Harare, September 1991.

an "electronic church" covering such cultural differences to develop "beliefs and practices which unite into one single" social internation-ally based "moral community ... all those who adhere to them," to use the Durkheimian definition of religion as a basis for collectivity.[52]

It is thus necessary to ask as did Philip Elliot: Is mass communica-tion at all possible? His findings indicated that in a given television production, the sources, producers and viewers operated out of their separate worlds, with little or no contact between them.[53] This may also be the case among the young women of Lamu and for the American televangelists' attempts to "save the world"[54] by means of satellites, cable networks, audio and video cassettes. Although there may be some feedback from a small portion of the audience to the sender organisation, *The 700 Club* in the United States in this instance, this is in our view far from constituting a common symbolic universe or a communication environment.

The 700 Club

A typical trait of *The 700 Club* is the instrumental significance at-tributed to *The 700 Club* itself in peoples' healing or religious experi-ences. Stylistically, this is obtained by the initial sequence resembling a docu drama followed by a studio interview with the person or per-sons in question. Various standard elements of advertisements for *The 700 Club* itself intermingle with the other elements of the programme, often appearing to "fill time." Concluding prayers by the hosts, most typically Pat Robertson himself, close *The 700 Club*, usually accompanied by additional invitations to "call or write our office in your country, today."[55]

The edition of *The 700 Club* used in our study is a typical example of the 30 minute programmed aired on ZBC. The main topic is vari-ous aspects of healing, or as Pat Robertson proclaims in his opening statement: "We are going to have an incredible miracle, we're going

---

52. Durkheim, 1968: 47.

53. Elliott, 1972. See also Høyer, 1991.

54. See, for instance, Schultze, 1990, or Bruce, 1990.

55. *The 700 Club*, taped from ZBC at various times during 1991.

to have a chance to pray for you, for your needs and we'll be expecting miracles for you."56

The edition opens with the only true international content of the programme, the opening sequence which consists of footage of people of different ethnic origins and in clearly different geographical settings. The female co-host introduces the main story of the day before the voice-over of a man recounting his son's accident. This leads to one of *The 700 Club's* most significant characteristics: the dramatisation of the story as it is being told. Today's story about the alleged healing of the young boy after an accident is dramatised and told to a reporter by the family involved. The parents claim the word of God as the healing agent: "After nine hours, God spoke."57 "I knew that God had heard our prayer. I knew he was coming out of that valley."58 To give the story more credibility, cuts from a family video are included.

The parents are later interviewed by Pat Robertson himself in front of a studio audience. In the course of the programme we learn that this is not the only healing the family has experienced, but it is the only healing which is "documented" by footage. The programme concludes following a prayer, a religious "commercial" for the Bible, and the standard closing remarks mentioned above. *The 700 Club* commences very much resembling a newscast, continues as a cross between a talk show and a magazine, and concludes as a programme-length commercial for *The 700 Club's* activities.59

We thus see that not only does the programme contain a set number of elements, the contents of each element is roughly the same from edition to edition. In our view, there is not much indication to justify the name "international" in the title. The technological optimism inherent in the view of television which made it such a popular medium for missionary organisations to spread their activities around the world, can also be seen in this use of television. The as-

---

56. Pat Robertson on *The 700 Club*, taped from ZBC in June 1991, © CBN 1990.

57. Voice of reporter, *The 700 Club*.

58. Words of the father of an injured boy, *The 700 Club* taped from ZBC in June 1991, © CBN 1990.

59. A more detailed discussion of *The 700 Club* as a television program will not be included in this paper, but will be included in the thesis of which this paper is a preliminary discussion.

sumption seems to be that Christianity can be spread around the globe like a consumer product.[60]

Television can be characterised by the concept of flow.[61] Audiences will typically attend to several messages from the medium in sequence, rather than specific segments or programmes as one would do with a literary text such as a novel. As the Danish media researcher Klaus Bruhn Jensen maintains: "A viewer does not watch programs, he or she watches television."[62] The viewer is exposed to different media messages, together constituting a super flow,[63] where the impact of one particular programme may be mingled with the symbolic content of other media messages. The polysemy of the message also gives rise to several different meanings within the same text. The hegemony of the programme itself is thus never total, as the struggle for meaning goes on all the time.[64] In this view, it is questionable whether one single programme poses any particular threat to a viewer or a culture. What is important however, is the collective impact media messages from other communication environments have on a viewer or receiving culture.

The audience

In order to test our hypothesis of the non-existing communication environment, we conducted interviews with several groups of respondents about their reactions to *The 700 Club*.[65] It may be argued that university students are not representative of the general Zimbabwean population. That is of course true. The students are, on the other hand, used to articulate their views and impressions in group discussions. In addition, they are used to watching television,

---

60. Schultze, 1990.
61. Williams, 1975.
62. Bruhn Jensen, 1989.
63. Bruhn Jensen, 1989.
64. Fiske, 1987: 93.

65. The students were grouped according to religious involvement. Each group consisted of three to six students, some groups of men and women separately, and some mixed groups. After showing a video recording of one episode of *The 700 Club*, up to two hours were spent discussing the students' impressions of the programme. Our interviews could of course not take the overall television flow into account, as only one recording was shown to the interviewees.

and they are familiar with the general codes for interpreting meaning of the symbolic content and format of television, in short, they are television literate. It was not our intention to make the groups representative of society at large, but rather to get a grip on the social and cultural processes behind the interpretation of the programmes in question. The interviews in the student community in Harare provided us with an opportunity to investigate this.[66]

The 700 Club as a communication environment

Although only some of our interviewees watched the programme on a regular basis, almost everybody had watched the programme at some point. Considering the distribution of television sets in Zimbabwe and the time the programme is aired, the viewing rate was higher than expected. When assessing the programme in terms of its communication environment, it is amazing how clearly the respondents perceive the programme as intended for an American audience. The hosts are interpreted as speaking not to them, but rather to people in the United States or to people of European origin living in Zimbabwe.[67] It is interesting to note how the concept of "the other" thus comes into the discussion. The hosts are not perceived as communicating to the respondents' environment, the programme is not perceived as intended for them, and although they identify the religious messages, the majority of the respondents interviewed regard the programme first and foremost as American entertainment. Let us merely give a few examples. Clearly, the appearances of the people portrayed in the programme make it stand out as American. The women group compares the programme to a women's fashion magazine portraying people before and after a complete takeover in clothes, hairstyle, make-up etc.[68] The programme will typically portray people with problems, which are solved when they become Christians: the troubles of "the before" are portrayed just as black and white as the "before" pictures in a fashion magazine, at the same time as the "after "story will be as

---

66. As the main focus of this paper is not the audience interpretation of *The 700 Club*, only a few examples of audience reactions are included. A full treatment of this can be found in the forthcoming thesis.

67. Interview with female students, Harare, September 1991.

68 Interview with female students, Harare, September 1991.

colourful and positive as the completely made-up women in the magazines.

Several of our respondents made a note of the the fact that to them the docu drama functions in two ways; it first gave some credibility to the story told, as they could in a sense see it with their own eyes: "you're not drawn to someone who says Oh, I was basically a nice person, I didn't do this, I didn't do that, then one day I just decided I must be a Christian without anything dramatic,... whereas if something dramatic, something almost unbelievable, or almost impossible happens, then you think about it sort of serious...."[69] At a later stage, however, many of them started reflecting about whether this was the real thing or merely a "fake" using a scripted story for converting the viewers to religion: "[they] created a possible situation which they would use to convince ... one preached using any means: drama, anything ...."[70] Another remarked: "I thought ... that even when they were praying ... that they were simply acting,... I was not convinced...."[71]

One aspect which received comment from almost all our groups was *The 700 Club's* emphasis on the connection between spiritual and physical or financial well-being. As one woman commented that when one is healed or becomes a Christian, the programme portrays the person in a better light, "then you become a better person even materially and all that." Particularly of irrelevance to their situation were the statements such as "money does not matter."[72] One respondent summarises his reactions, "who is in the capacity to say that, if I don't have that money, I need the money. If you have everything, then ... it doesn't matter. But if I don't have the money, what matter is how do I get the money, how do I survive. One begins to wonder, the whole motifs, force behind that."

The respondents thus confirmed the view of John Fiske and others that the audience is actively decoding the television message. This is an example of the concepts of *preferred reading*.[73] The respondents recognise the intended message of the programme while at the same time turning the message around to make it suit their own purpose.

---

69. Interview with female students, Harare, September 1991.
70. Interview with male students, Harare, September 1991.
71. Interview with male students, Harare, September 1991.
72. Statement by interviewed woman portrayed on *The International 700 Club*.
73. Hall, 1980.

The students worded the intended message for instance as follows: "To get people to believe in the power of Jesus" or "That Jesus performs miracles to those who believe in him."[74] The viewers of these programmes may use the programmes as raw material for the handling of their personal situations within their social material field of action as was also the case with the women of Lamu and the Indian films. This was particularly the case for respondents who called themselves Christians: "It reminds me of my first day of revelation and being born again to Jesus."[75] Statements of this kind confirm studies done in the United States that the religious television message is most favourably received by the "already converted."[76]

Through such interpretation of the symbolic material, both the respondents in Harare and the women in Lamu demonstrated a resistance against foreign symbol products. There may thus be a great gap between the intended message from the producer's point of view and the message which the viewer extracts from the programme. Although he or she may see what is perceived to be the preferred reading, he or she may choose to interpret the symbolic content differently. It is thus too simple to equate the television text with the viewers' reading of the text, and thus say that television programming poses a cultural threat on the basis of the content alone.[77] It is thus necessary to modify the pessimistic picture of cultural imperialism or media imperialism while at the same time pointing out the absurdity of such symbolic content being broadcast world-wide.

It is, however, dangerous to dismiss the possible cultural influences as nonsense just because television studies have found that audiences to a large extent produce their own reading of media content. The programmes are nonetheless there, and they may eventually become a part of the culture by becoming a part of the symbolic content of the society in question. The reading of the content is, we must remember, made within the boundaries of the content itself.

Although *The 700 Club* in Zimbabwe may be a part of the system of media imperialism, the audience's active decoding of the messages may counter some of the negative influences. In our view, the clue in

---

74. Interview with mixed pilot group, Harare, September 1991.

75. Interview with a group of female non-students, Harare, September 1991.

76. See, for instance, Hoover, 1988.

77. Gentikow, 1989.

counteracting unwanted foreign influences from television does not only lie in import quotas or other political measures. As one of our respondents remarked: "I believe ... of course there should be this exchange, but it should be healthy."[78] The answer does rather lie in the audience's own powers of resistance towards and active reading of the content. As Liebes and Katz pointed out in their study of cross cultural readings of Dallas, "each pattern of involvement includes a mechanism of defense."[79] Although the reading of the text in question may be made within the hegemony of the text itself, the audiences seemed quite ready to rewrite the message to suit their particular situation or to dismiss the content as being entirely outside of their communication environment.

We would like to argue that *The 700 Club* in our view neither constitutes nor fits into a communication environment in Zimbabwe, nor is part of a transnational communication environment. It may be absurd that the term "electronic church" be used for a phenomenon which counters the basic Durkheimian definition of religion as "one single moral community."[80] What is more critical is that such media phenomena as the "electronic church" establish surrounding activities, the parachurch, to support the media messages. This combination of mass mediated and personal communication has, through communication research been shown to be more "effective" in determining people's attitudes and actions. But as far as the airing of the programmes themselves are concerned, our studies have confirmed our hypothesis that the audience is equipped with capabilities of rewriting the messages in their own terms based on their own cultural contexts, thereby rewriting the intended message and possibly counteracting the potential message from other cultural contexts. After all, "no one feels comfortable with someone else's junk."[81]

---

78. Interview with male students, Harare, September 1991.
79. Liebes & Katz, 1990: 128.
80. Durkheim, 1968: 47.
81. Interview with male students, Harare, September 1991.

Bibliography

Altheide, D.L. & Snow, R.P., 1979: *Media Logic*, Sage, Beverly Hills.
Berger, P. L., 1969: *The Sacred Canopy. Elements of a Sociological Theory of Religion*, Doubleday, New York.
Berger, P. L. & Luckmann, T., 1971: *The Social Construction of Reality. A Treatise in the Sociology of Knowledge*, Penguin Books, Harmondsworth (1966).
Bourdieu, P., 1977: *Outline of a Theory of Practice*, Cambridge University Press, Cambridge.
Bourdillon, M., 1990: *Religion and Society. A Text for Africa*, Mambo Press, Gweru.
Boyd-Barrett, O., 1977: "Media Imperialism: Towards an International Frame-work for the Analysis of Media Systems," in Curran, J; Gurevitch, M. & Wollacott, J. (eds), *Mass Communication and Society*, Edward Arnold, London.
Bruce, S., 1990: *Pray TV: Televangelism in America*, Routledge, London.
Bruhn Jensen, K., 1989: *Print Cultures and Visual Cultures, A Critical Introduction to a New Research Agenda*, Occasional papers from JMK, Department of Journalism, Media and Communication, University of Stockholm.
Chaney, D., 1986: "A Symbolic Mirror of Ourselves; Civic Ritual in Mass Society," in Collins, Richard et. al. (eds), *Media, Culture and Society: A Critical Reader*, Sage Publications, London.
Dahlgren, P., 1990: "TV och våra kulturella referensramar" ("Television and our Cultural Frames of Reference"), in Hannerz, Ulf (ed.), *Medier och Kulturer (Media and Cultures)*, Carlssons Bokförlag, Stockholm.
Daneel, I., 1987: *Quest for Belonging. Introduction to a Study of African Independent Churches*, Mambo Press, Gweru.
Durkheim, E., 1968: *The Elementary, Forms of the Religious Life*, Allen & Unwin, London (1912).
Elliott, P., 1972: *The Making of a Television Series. A Case Study in the Sociology of Culture*, Constable, London.
Featherstone, M. (ed.), 1990: *Global Culture. Nationalism, Globalization and Modernity*, Sage, London & Newbury Park & New Dehli.
Fiske, J., 1982: *Introduction to Communication Studies*, Methuen, London.
Fiske, J., 1987: *Television Culture*, Methuen, London.
Fortner, R., 1990: "Saving the World? American Evangelicals and Transnational Broadcasting," in Schultze, Q. (ed), *American Evangelicals and the Mass Media*, Academie Books, Grand Rapids.
Frankl, R., 1987: *Televanglism: The Marketing of Popular Religion*, Southern Illinois University Press, Carbondale.
Fuglesang, M., 1990: "Film som romantikens verktyg: Om medialisering i staden Lamu, Kenya" ("Film as the tool of Romanticism"), in Hannerz, U, (ed.), *Medier och Kulturer*, (Media and Cultures), Carlssons Bokförlag, Stockholm.
Gentikow, B., 1989: *Mister dansk kultur sin identitet i massemediernes internationalisering?* Working paper number 35, Centre for Cultural Research, University of Aarhus, Denmark.
Giddens, A., 1989: *Sociology*, Polity Press, Cambridge.

Hall, S., 1980: "Encoding/Decoding," in Hall, S; Hobson, D; Lowe, A. and Willis, P. (eds), *Culture, Media Language*, London, Hutchinson.

Harrell, D.E. Jr, 1987: *Pat Robertson: A Personal, Political and Religious Portrait*, Harper & Row, San Francisco.

Hoover, S., 1988: *Mass Media Religion, The Social Sources of the Electronic Church*, Sage, Newbury Park.

Høyer, S.,1991: "According to Media Research—Does Mass Communication Work?," in Rønning, Helge & Lundby, Knut (eds.), *Media and Communication. Readings in Methodology, History and Culture*, Norwegian University Press (Universitetsforlaget), Oslo/Oxford University Press.

Lee, C., 1980: *Media Imperialism Reconsidered: The Homogenizing of Media Culture*, Sage Publications, London.

Liebes, T. & Katz, E., 1990: *The Export of Meaning: Cross Cultural Readings of Dallas*, Oxford University Press, Oxford.

Lundby, K, & Rønning, H., 1991: "Media-Culture-Communication: Modernity Interpreted Through Media Culture," in Rønning, Helge & Lundby, Knut (eds.), *Media and Communication. Readings in Methodology, History and Culture*, Norwegian University Press (Universitetsforlaget), Oslo/ Oxford University Press.

Lundby, K., 1992: *Mediekultur* (Media Culture), Department of Media and Communication, University of Oslo.

Melkote, S. R., 1991: *Communication for Development in the Third World. Theory and Practice*, Sage, New Delhi.

Murdock, G. & Golding, P., 1977: "Capitalism, Communication and Class Relations," in J. Curran et al (eds.), *Mass Communication and Society*, London.

Nugdalla, S. A., 1986: "Broadcasting and Cultural Change," in Wedell, George (ed.), *Making Broadcasting Useful: The African Experience The Development of Radio and Television in Africa in the 1980s*, Manchester University Press/ European Institute for the Media, Manchester.

Robertson, R., 1990: "Mapping the Global Condition: Globalization as the Central Concept," in Featherstone, Mike (ed.), *Global Culture. Nationalism, Globalization and Modernity*, Sage, London & Newbury Park & New Delhi.

Schultze, Q., 1990: "Defining the Electronic Church," in Abelman, R. & Hoover, S. (eds), *Religious Television: Controversies and Conclusions*, Ablex Publishing Corporation, Norwood, New Jersey.

Schultze, Q. J., 1987: *The Mythos of the Electronic Church*, Critical Studies in Mass Communication, 4, 245–261.

Tunstall, J., 1977: *The Media are American*, New York, Columbia University Press.

Tvedt, T., 1990: *Bilder av de andre: Om utviklingslandene i bistandsepoken*, (Images of the Others: The Developing Countries in the Era of Development Aid), Universitetsforlaget, Oslo.

Varis, T., 1974: "Global Traffic in Television," *Journal of Communication*, 24, 107.

Waldahl, R., 1991: "Political Attitudes and Public Opinion," in Rønning, Helge & Lundby, Knut (eds.), *Media and Communication. Readings in Methodology, History and Culture*, Norwegian University Press (Universitetsforlaget), Oslo/ Oxford University Press.

Williams, R., 1975: *Television. Technology and Cultural Form*, Schocken Books, New York.

Østerberg, D., 1990: "Det sosio-materielle handlingsfelt" ("The Social Material Field of Action") in Deicman-Sørensen, T, & Frønes, I (eds.), *Kulturanalyse* (Cultural Analysis), Gyldendal, Oslo.

Zimbabwe: One State, One Faith, One Lord

Chenjerai Hove

"Every revolution tends to worship its leaders," says Octavio Paz, the Mexican poet and essayist. Later, when those prayers make Gods out of our leaders, a certain type of citizen is created. Paz described the one-state citizen well: "He shuts himself away to protect himself; his face is a mask and so is his smile."

In a one-party state, the citizen lives in solitude and, according to Paz, "everything serves as a defence: silence and words, politeness and disdain, irony and resignation." Thus we end up with a falsified human being who is conveniently subservient, artificially humble, deceptive in word and deed. In other words, very unpredictable. These features can be seen in many one-party states, most of which are busy unburdening themselves today.

Politicians must rule through the people's political, social and cultural goodwill, not through compulsion and force. No nation can thrive on compulsion for long.

The one-party state is born out of the notion of father. "No family can have two fathers," they say. Thus one nation, one leader was born. The father myth is transposed to the political realm, with many consequences unconducive to the welfare of the state.

Zimbabwe recently went through an election in which the ruling party won nearly all the parliamentary seats available. The behaviour and assumptions of our politicians as they campaigned during the elections help us to understand the political culture we are developing.

At some point I decided that I would never vote in my life, especially when a senior politician claimed that Africans were not yet mature enough for multi-party democracy. Another senior politician claimed on television that Zimbabwe could do with a second-best Constitution simply because our Constitution is better than most third world Constitutions. But then I said no, I will vote, or even spoil my vote. Then I started to think seriously about the ways of the African politician as he chews words and hurls insults at both voter and political opponent. Certain characteristics of our leaders began to have meaning, to show me the way Africa will go for a long time unless a new type of politician is born.

Why, for example, do African leaders mistake a critic for an enemy in any discussion of national issues? Why do African leaders get offended if anyone criticises them or their policies? Why do African leaders relish empty praise by praise-singers and sycophants? Why do our leaders allow flattery to be their diet in the media?

The birth of the sycophant, the praise-singer, the hanger-on, is a culture of those who do not want to risk their lives through sincerity and honesty. In the end, they are usually the ones who are best positioned to write the biography of the nation's leader, and so the praise-singer at the chief's court goes on *ad infinitum*, forward to the century of chieftaincies and feudal lords, in this age of technology and critical thinking.

African leaders get angry when criticised. Their anger explodes through those who are employed to get angry on behalf of the President or the military ruler. Instead of examining the ideas of the critic, they rush quickly for the critic's throat, armed with threats and imprisonment.

One of the reasons they get angry when criticised is that they have this chain of praise-singers and sycophants who give them the impression that if they had not been around, the country would collapse. They never entertain the notion that in every country there are as many potential leaders as the population of that country. Politics is the only profession which does not require any entry qualifications, as Papandreou of Greece admitted.

Another possible reason that African leaders lose their temper when confronted with criticism is that they do not have many original ideas. Imagine an African head of state spending the people's money building Saint Peter's Basilica in an African country. Our own case is the national sports stadium, which no one seems willing to use, so it lies idle. Then we have this vast dream of a massive Parliament; when you hear politicians praise it, you would think the building itself will speak instead of the parliamentarians. And there will be talk of canals where there are not even seas or rivers, and huge aeroplanes to earn foreign currency when the national airline is running at a loss all the time.

For most African leaders, talk of retirement is an insult, a treasonable act for which an honest citizen can be hanged. Their main reason for not wanting to retire is that they offend so much when they are in power that they fear a possible investigation should they leave power. The one-party state is convenient as an institution of monopolising power, legitimising it so that it is seen to be constitutional. It also had to do with fame: *The Guinness Book of Records* for the longest-reigning ruler. Musaemura Zimunya was right about one of our acquisitions from Europe: the prison. I wonder what it feels like for a leader who wants to be considered great, to lock up a critic for some flimsy offence of words or a demonstration. Africa has the misfortune of being ruled with more brutality than persuasion. The people are only a means to an end—power. Look at what is done in the name of the people—repression and suppression of alternative views, huge loans they have no idea how to repay, weird agreements with foreign governments for the most weird purposes, building huge showcase structures which the people stare at from a distance in utter disbelief and fear.

Our media must stop the praise songs. Advisers to our leaders must know that they are accountable to the people, not to the whims of the rulers. African politicians must move away from the concept of being beggars parading around the world asking for huge loans which no one has the slightest idea how to repay. And for cultural workers, writers, musicians, poets, dancers, the temptation to become a praise-singer is high. Some have already done it, others will do it, some did it and gave up, tired of the monotony of sycophancy and praise-singing, tired of the art of flattery since it is repetitive and uninspiring.

I look forward to an African leader whom I can meet in the street, with a loaf of well-priced bread under my arm, to challenge him on his budget speech the previous day, while he challenges me on the literary merit of my latest bad novel or poem. In the end, I will say to him, you have done well, but let's do better; he will say to me, continue writing even if I do not agree with your literary products, it is good to have them. And he and I will agree.

Rich and Poor Languages in Botswana

Lars-Gunnar Andersson and Tore Janson

This chapter presents an overview of the situation pertaining to the languages of Botswana. The point of the chapter is to elaborate on the concept of rich and poor languages with particular reference to the use of language in literature, or to express it more modestly: the use of language in writing.

The concept *developing language* is introduced and characterized below. This concept is tailored in such a way that it fits Setswana, the national language of Botswana, more or less perfectly. The interesting thing about this language is that it is moving from the category of poor languages into the family of rich languages. During this process we call it a developing language.

The move from poor to rich in the world of languages is not a deterministic or inevitable process. Rather it is a process dependent on conscious efforts on the part of the speech community, such as the language policy of the country and the attitude towards the language among its speakers.

The arguments given are almost totally restricted to the languages of Botswana. Further facts about that country and its languages can be found in Janson and Tsonope (1991) and Andersson and Janson (forthcoming). The scope of the chapter is, however, wider. There are parallel processes in several other parts of the world, not least in Africa. In fact, we would claim that the concept of developing language and the distinction between rich and poor languages are relevant for most countries in Africa south of the Sahara.[1]

There are several kinds of inequalities among the world's languages. For one thing, some are spoken by millions and some by just a few thousand. One obvious way to measure the strength or the richness of a language is, of course, in terms of the number of speakers. However, this is not what we intend to do in this chapter. Rather

---

1. For further reading about these aspects of African languages, see Cyffer and others (1991) and the Unesco survey of African community languages (1985).

we will focus on how well endowed the language is when it comes to written material and tools needed for the use of the language in writing.

There are, as we see it, linguistic, literary and educational aspects of the richness or the strength of a language. The situation in Botswana will be discussed with respect to these three aspects.

Languages in Botswana—the basic facts

Botswana, situated adjacent to the northern border of South Africa, has about 1.3 million inhabitants. The area is as large as that of France, but most of the country's surface is covered by the Kalahari desert. Most people live in the south-eastern part of the country, where there are reasonable conditions for agriculture.

Setswana, a language of the Bantu family, is the mother tongue of approximately 80 per cent of the population. Of the others, perhaps 10 per cent speak Ikalanga, another Bantu language; the remaining 10 per cent speak one of approximately 20 small minority languages, belonging to the Bantu or Khoisan families. Setswana is spoken all over the country, while Ikalanga is used in the east, along the border with Zimbabwe, and the many small languages are found mainly in and around the desert, and in the Okavango delta in the far north-west. This means that the small minority groups tend to live in the poorest and most remote areas of the country.

English, the former colonial language, is used extensively in administration and education, and is designated as the official language of the country. Setswana is often referred to as the national language in official contexts.

Let us now turn our attention to the three different aspects of richness of a language mentioned above.

The linguistic aspect

The first thing that comes to mind in discussing the linguistic aspect of richness in written material is the existence of an orthography for the language, i.e. a system for transferring the sounds of the language into letters of the alphabet. The construction of an orthography presupposes linguistic knowledge. Today it is rather easy to set up orthographies for the Bantu languages spoken in southern Africa. The reason is that a tradition of how to construct orthographies for the Bantu languages has been established through the work of many linguists in the last hundred years or so. The only sensible technique today is to construct new orthographies according to the principles of already existing orthographies.

However, this does not mean that all the details of the orthographies are easy to set up. Questions and uncertainties will always arise as all languages have their share of linguistic peculiarities. For every language, there must be situations where one does not know which way to go, where one solution appears to be as good as another. However, a decision has to be made. This means that to a considerable extent, an orthography is arbitrary and has to be accepted as a convention.

An orthography is a necessary linguistic tool for using a language in writing, but it is not all that is needed. A dictionary which provides the writers with words, spellings and inflections is also necessary, not in theory but in practice. Furthermore, a set of principles regulating punctuation and similar things is more or less necessary. Let us give one example of a rule of this type. In all Bantu languages there is a rich system of concord particles. If the subject of a sentence belongs to class 1 (and all nouns of the language belong to a certain noun class), then there should be a class 1 concord particle in front of the predicate. Should this particle be written together with the predicate verb (conjunctive writing) or should it be written as a separate word (disjunctive writing)? The answer to this question is not obvious and there are reasonable arguments for both positions. However, a publisher of books, newspapers or magazines has to take a stand on this question. For practical reasons it should not be an issue each time an author writes down a sentence.

Furthermore, a grammar of the language is needed. The language has to be codified in some way. We could say that a grammar gives a characterization of the language. This characterization or description is always an idealization of the living reality where every language is used in thousands of different ways. It is unrealistic to have a grammar which does not allow any variations among the speakers, and it is equally unrealistic to have a grammar which accepts all variations existing in the speech community. Among other things we can say that a grammar defines a language (or a standard for the language) and sets it apart from other languages.

In short, an orthography, a dictionary, a grammar and a set of principles for writing are necessary for the successful use of a language as a written language. All three embody a large number of conventions on which the language users have to agree for practical reasons.

In Botswana, English is the official language and Setswana the national language. For English all the linguistic tools that one could possibly need are available. It stands as a prototype for the rich language. The situation for Setswana is considerably less fortunate. There are and have been for some time a standard orthography, a grammar and a couple of dictionaries. In other words, the tools that are necessary for using the language in written form do exist. This does not mean that it would not be a good thing to have more grammatical descriptions and more dictionaries. For example, there is no comprehensive monolingual dictionary, only dictionaries to and from English and Afrikaans. Further, grammars and dictionaries have mostly not been written by native speakers of the language.

On the other hand, in comparison to the minority languages of Botswana, Setswana is a rather rich language. For the minority languages, more or less everything is wanting—orthographies, grammars, dictionaries and everything else. We shall not specify what has been written about these different languages through the years. Let us just say that the literature in and about these languages varies between zero pages and perhaps a few hundred pages. Further, in most cases when studies of different languages have been made the purpose has not been to construct practical tools which would help the speakers in using the language in writing. Typical publications are either linguistic notes, written for the benefit of other linguists, or translations of the Bible and other works emanating from the activity of missionaries.

The literary aspect

For any familiar European language, linguistic works are only a tiny fraction of the total number of printed texts, including for example official texts, religious texts, newspapers and magazines, and literary or artistic works (novels, short stories, detective stories, science fiction, poetry and everything else). On the other hand the linguistic works (orthography, dictionary etc.) are logically and sometimes also temporally prior to the general use of a language in print.

In Setswana, the number of printed texts is still fairly low, and the ones that are found belong to only a few areas. Official texts like laws, memoranda, proclamations, minutes from meetings etc. exist only to a very limited extent. In such contexts, English is used almost exclusively. The same is true for business correspondence, invoices and many other everyday documents.

The field where Setswana is used most consistently is that of Christian religion. The English missionaries, who started their work in the 1820s, were the first to use the language in writing. The whole Bible was translated into Setswana more than 100 years ago, and there are many other religious texts. Almost all are translations.

Newspapers and magazines in Botswana are preponderantly in English. The government publishes a newspaper and a magazine, which are both bilingual, but other newspapers mostly use English, with occasional chapters in Setswana.

The use of a language in literature is a measure of the richness of the language. In a multilingual society some languages, or maybe just one, will be used more in literature than others. In Botswana, as in many other former colonies, most of the literature is written in the old colonial language—in this case in English.

There are a few things published in Setswana—short stories, poems and traditional tales, for example. So far, no full-scale novel has been written in Setswana. The literary production of Botswana is still mostly carried out in English. The books are written in English, and they are discussed and reviewed in English.

There are also very few translations into Setswana. Naturally, this is to a large extent due to economic factors, but it also seems that the people who read books overwhelmingly prefer to read in English rather than in their mother tongue.

The educational aspect

By the educational aspect of the richness of a language we mean the extent to which it is used in education.

Of all the world's languages just a few per cent can take a person all the way through the educational system from first grade to a university degree. If a language is used as a medium of instruction at all levels of the educational system, it is quite obvious that this means a lot for the strength and the vitality of the language.

The situation in Botswana is the following. For most children Setswana is the language of the school for the first four years. They learn how to read and write in Setswana and English is only studied as a subject. After these four years English comes in as a medium of instruction.

One can argue at length about the number of years that children should use their mother tongue at school. There is no one accepted and uncontroversial answer, and we will not go into the possible arguments for different points of view. The situation in Botswana is comparable to that in many African countries. What we can say is that if Setswana were to be used more extensively in education, more books written in Setswana have to be published. In all probability, the terminology for different fields of study like history, geography, mathematics etc. would have to be further developed. At present, many terms for scientific concepts are only available in English. However, it is not an impossible task to produce the terminology in Setswana. It would make the education and the books more expensive, but if the result would be that that the students understood the subjects faster and better, this procedure might pay off within a limited amount of time. This linguistic aspect of the educational system of Botswana is, as we see it, extremely interesting. Will English continue to be the totally dominating language in the schools of Botswana, or will the role of Setswana be strengthened—and if it is strengthened, to what extent will that be?

An interesting indicator of trends is the status of English schools, where English is the medium of instruction from the start. Only few such schools exist, mainly in the capital, Gaborone. They are frequented by the children of those who have English as their first language, but also by people who have other European or Asian languages as their first language. Furthermore, it is not unusual for well educated Batswana (at least in Gaborone) to place their children in an English school. This shows that the English schools and/or the English language enjoy high prestige.

A few words should be said about the role of the different minority languages in the educational system of the country. These languages are not used at all. Even in areas where more or less all children have Ikalanga or some other minority language as their mother tongue, only Setswana and English are used in school. In this respect the educational policy of Botswana is very nationalistic—the national language Setswana is promoted at the expense of all the other African languages used within the country. The different local languages are totally neglected.

In this context, we may point out that the plans of the neighbouring and newly independent Namibia is quite different. There the different local languages are suggested to be used during the first three years of schooling, and after that the official language English should be introduced as medium of instruction. We must point out that the language policy of Namibia so far only exists on paper. It has not yet been implemented in the schools—a procedure which will take considerable time and effort. Among other things, books are needed as well as teachers competent in the different languages they will have to use in the future. We make this point about Namibia mainly to show that there certainly are alternatives to the present policy of the Botswana school system.

Setswana—a developing language

Let us define a developing language as a language where the body of literature—everything that has been written and printed in the language—amounts to between five and fifty feet of book shelf space. This definition should not be taken too seriously, it is just a very simple way of operationalizing the concept of developing language. The idea is that some languages are in the process of establishing themselves as written languages with a non-negligible production of printed texts.

Setswana is precisely such a language. Today books written in Setswana could fill an ordinary size book case. This is not very much but the interesting thing is that much of it has been produced in the last few years. This situation calls for attention. Setswana could very well within a decade or two develop into a language which is used extensively in books, newspapers and magazines. There is a growing strength in the language.

Yet most of the authors, journalists and academics write in English today and many, maybe all, write with less effort in English than in their mother tongue Setswana. They are not used to expressing themselves in Setswana when it comes to writing and when it comes to subjects like politics, economics, culture or linguistics.

For a young author to write in English is a far better way to fame and success than to write in Setswana. The only internationally well-known author from Botswana is Bessie Head (who was born and grew up in South Africa), and she wrote in English.

For the language(s) and culture(s) of Botswana and other countries in Southern Africa it would certainly be advantageous if more literary works were written in the indigenous languages. From a linguistic point of view the literary heroes of Southern Africa are those who write in the African languages. Unfortunately there is not much incentive to do so. It is quite clear that reviewers and other key figures in the international literary world pay their attention to those who write in English. They are the ones who are invited to conferences and congresses. Whether this situation will change in the future, we do not know, but we do think it essential that it does. For a language like Setswana, which is on its way into a modern technological world, it is essential to bring with it high quality works describing the life, thoughts and wisdom of the traditional culture of Botswana. Such descriptions must be written in Setswana, so that the reader can experience what the people actually said, not just an account in a foreign language of what they said.

For every book or newspaper chapter that is written in Setswana, the next one will be a little bit easier to write. It is, of course, a strange and somewhat unnatural situation when it is easier to write in a second than in a first language. This illustrates the importance of practice and tradition.

Neglected languages

The fact that there are about twenty minority languages in one country may strike many Europeans as unusual and something which must create problems for the language policy. However, the really striking thing about Botswana in an African perspective is that it is so linguistically homogenous. There is one dominating language, Setswana, spoken as a first language by around 80 percent of the population. Promoting Setswana as the national language is a rather natural thing to do in a situation like this.

On the other hand, promoting a language does not necessarily mean that all other languages should be totally forgotten. This is, unfortunately, more or less the case in Botswana. There is an obvious lack of interest in the minority languages, both politically and academically. The minority languages are neglected from linguistic, literary and pedagogical points of view. There seems to be little interest in developing orthographies, dictionaries and grammars for these languages. No works are written and the languages are not used in education. By all standards mentioned here, these languages are poor languages. That is, they are poor in the sense that they lack the things needed for the use of the languages in writing. They are certainly not poor when it comes to grammatical complexity and other aspects of the linguistic structure: in those respects, all natural languages are on a similar level.

For the only major minority language Ikalanga, which is spoken by around ten percent of the population, independence in 1966 actually meant a step back. Ikalanga was used earlier as the medium of instruction in some missionary schools in north-eastern Botswana.

When we have discussed language policy with Ikalanga speakers, it becomes quite clear that they would like to see a promotion of the Ikalanga language. For example, all the students we have interviewed hold the view that Ikalanga should be the language that one learns to read and write first.

What we have said above about the importance of literary works being published in Setswana can, of course, also be said about all the different minority languages of the country. On the other hand, in these cases it is, as far as we can see, not likely that a literary tradition will develop (with the possible exception of the Ikalanga language). What one can hope is that individual enthusiasts will document their own mother tongues in writing.

Modern technology is present in Botswana and with the help of word processors and copying machines publishing in more modest and inexpensive ways becomes possible. This means that individuals and groups of individuals could do quite a few things to promote their mother tongues within the community.

Writing without a written language

Even if the language policy of the country gives the minority language speakers no support, there are a few things they can do themselves, if they want to promote their language. They can or rather they must use their mother tongue when talking to members of the same group. They can also use their mother tongue in writing. This can be done even if there is no orthography for the language. For non-official purposes a language can be used in writing, even if the language does not have a written form. This may seem like a contradiction at first, but it is nevertheless possible.

If you are an educated person in Botswana, you have learnt to read and write in Setswana. The orthography for Setswana is a rather modern product, which means that the system for transferring sounds into letters of the alphabet is fairly transparent. Therefore a minority language speaker can use the same principles for writing his or her mother tongue. Essentially this means that you borrow the Setswana orthography and use it (as well as you can) for your own language. The closer this other language is related to Setswana, the easier this will be. Thus we should point out that this is much easier for the Bantu languages than for the Khoisan languages, in which for example the click sounds by necessity create problems for the writer.

We have seen some very nice examples of this type of writing without a written language. We possess, for example, a copy of a letter written in Sekgalagadi, a language without a written language, i.e. without an orthography. This letter was part of a correspondence between a sister and a brother. We suspect that this use of minority languages in writing occurs now and then in Botswana.

This type of individual support for the minority languages is promising. It gives some hope for the future. Furthermore, without this type of individual enthusiasm, pride and effort, the most probable prospect for the future is that these languages will disappear within a few generations.

The future of Setswana

In colonial times, Botswana, or Bechuanaland as it was then called, was officially dominated by English, in that English was the administrative language, but it was certainly not the majority language. Rather most people spoke their mother tongues and only occasionally did they come into contact with English. Literacy was low, and most people did not attend school at all.

Educational reforms have increased knowledge of English immensely. Today well over 80 per cent of the young people attend school, where they become literate in both Setswana and English.

But, still, the great majority of the population are more skilled in Setswana than in English. Obviously, this holds for all those whose first language is Setswana, but it is also a fact that most people who have Sesubiya, Seyeyi, Otjiherero, Ikalanga etc. as their first language find it easier to speak Setswana than English. One reason for this is that Setswana is the major lingua franca of the country, i.e. the language used in communication between people who do not have the same mother tongue. English is also used as a lingua franca in Botswana, especially when foreigners are involved, but it is not at all used as much as Setswana in the contacts between different language groups.

English still is called the official language of the country, but in shops and bars and in market places all around the country Setswana is the language used. Up to very recently, English was the only language spoken in Parliament. This has just been changed, and it is now possible to use Setswana as well in the debates in the Parliament. There are good reasons for this change. Many members of Parliament find it easier to express themselves in Setswana than in English. More importantly, most citizens find it easier to follow a discussion in Setswana than in English. Because of that, this shift from English into Setswana in the political sphere is beneficial for democracy.

The language of conversation used in the Government's office buildings and the different ministries and departments, i.e. in the corridors of power, nowadays is mostly Setswana. This represents a change from earlier decades, when the presence of a high proportion of foreign experts made it necessary to use English as the everyday language.

The relative strength between English and Setswana can be studied at the university. English dominates totally when it comes to writing, almost a hundred per cent. In academic teaching, English dominates as well. Sometimes the professor is a foreigner who knows English but not Setswana, and in many cases there are students with a European or Asian background who do not know Setswana. But if there is a class where all participants know both languages, then they will use both English and Setswana. English is used more than Setswana, and the principle seems to be that when the discussion touches on more local, private and personal things, Setswana comes in. In the discussions among students on the campus, Setswana is used more than English.

We could go through one area of social life after another and discuss the relative strength between Setswana and English. We will not do this, but we would like to point out some aspects of the pattern that would emerge if this was done.

English clearly dominates in writing and Setswana equally clearly dominates the spoken language. We have met several foreigners in Botswana complaining about the constant use of spoken Setswana in areas of social life where they had the preconception that the official language English would be used. Some of them are Europeans working for the UN or some foreign aid organisation. Others are well educated Africans from neighbouring countries like Zambia and Zimbabwe who find it hard to work as physicians, for example, when both staff and patients mostly speak Setswana. Some of them say that people should try to speak English, since English, after all, is the official language.

One could, of course, turn the argument around and say that Setswana should be given the status of official language, since it is already used as one. If we look at the facts of language use, then we could say that there are two official languages in Botswana. English is the official language in writing and Setswana the official language in speech.

In the future it could very well be the case that there will be a shift in favour of Setswana. In order for this to be the case, it is essential that Setswana is further developed as a written language. More articles and books have to be written, and journalistic and literary traditions need to be developed. As we have pointed out above, there are both democratic and cultural arguments for encouraging journalists, authors, teachers, administrators and politicians to use Setswana in writing.

Today Setswana is a developing language. In the future it will, in all likelihood, be a rich language. The real question is whether this will take one, two or perhaps three decades. In any case, Setswana will soon apply for membership of the league of rich languages.

Bibliography

Andersson, L.-G. & Janson, T. (forthcoming). *Languages in Botswana.*

Anonymous (1985). *African community languages and their use in literacy and education.* Dakar: Unesco Regional Office for Education in Africa.

Cyffer, N., Schubert, K., Weier, H.-I., & Wolf, E. (eds.) (1991). *Language Standardization in Africa / Sprachstandardisierung in Afrika / Standardisation des langues en Afrique.* Hamburg: Buske.

Janson, T., & Tsonope, J. (1991). *Birth of a National Language: The History of Setswana.* Gaborone: Heinemann Botswana.

Ong, W. J. (1982). *Orality and Literacy: The Technologizing of the Word.* London and New York: Methuen.

Living in the Neighbourhood of One's Dreams: The Role of Popular Writing in the Creation of the Ordinary

Bodil Folke Frederiksen

On the final page of his novel, *The Price of Living*, the Kenyan writer Yussuf K. Dawood refers to all of the two hundred and fifty preceding pages as "this make-believe world" (Dawood 1983: 168). His last minute subversion of his own text has intrigued me for some time. I take it to refer not only to novels being fiction, but also to suggest that his text constitutes a fantastic world—or a fantasy. To a European reader the novel is very far from fantasy—there is nothing magic about it, it is drably realistic and everyday, much concerned with its main characters' professional lives, consumption patterns and the interior decoration of offices and houses. What Dawood seems to be doing in his work is rather a creation of the ordinary, incorporating and repeating words and phrases useful in the description of modern living; a familiarisation exercise: "'This way, sir,' the medical secretary said as she led Maina Karanja into the Executive Clinic." "Executive" is full of longing for a weighty and orderly existence, as is Mr. Karanja's subsequent prim compliment to the secretary, Miss Collins: "Impeccable organisation as usual" (Dawood 1983: 13). The whole novel is a utopia of the ordinary, and in an African context that makes its universe "a make-believe world."

For urban Africans, an everyday and comfortable life, free of misery and harassment, is an adventure. The opposite is the norm. The implication of this for popular literature is that what is dismissed as fairly humdrum descriptive realism in western literature, is fantastic in an African context. Many popular novels from Kenya, Tanzania, and Nigeria may best be seen as realistic fantasies, meticulously describing the lives of the fabulously rich. Or the lives of the not so rich in terms of their efforts to grab and enjoy a modern lifestyle, closely associated with consumer goods, amenities and leisure, but also with regular work and the ability to afford school fees.

The ordinary is the utopia. But in a dynamic situation the ordinary has to be imagined and constructed. In this creative process popular arts and popular culture more broadly play a key role. In areas of popular culture issues central to the everyday life of the majority of the population are being articulated and debated; new discursive practices appear, and new modes of life are made visible, audible, and thinkable.

In Africa cities are the locus of what is modern. They are hotbeds of social and cultural change, and the turmoil characteristic of all levels of African urban life finds expression in a multitude of popular culture genres, which are themselves changeable and evanescent. Aspirations are formed and utopias imagined in a context of a multitude of innovating cultural practices and institutions. They set the parametres and define the discourses within which cultural change, including social betterment, happens. Important cultural practices which predominate in urban areas include writing and print (fiction, newspapers, magazines), visual media (film, television, video and advertising), multi-linguism (for Kenya: English, Swahili, Arabic, various Indian languages, sub-national African languages). And they reflect and are fed by modern social and cultural institutions: bureaucracies, agencies of control (police and army), formal and informal institutions of education and training, international development agencies, tourism, conspicuous consumption, sports events, bars, entertainment, and night life.

Urban life and written culture, particularly novels and magazines, belong together. Historically this has been the case in Europe, and it is the case in Africa. From the point of view of the production of printed material the appropriate social organisation of technology and communication infrastructure is present in towns. From that of consumption the scale and density of the population in towns make possible the creation of a public or mass audience. The transition from "community" to "public" is in itself a sign of a significant change, implying lateral organisation of anonymous equivalent individuals, and a principle of social organisation radically different from that of communities, characterized by being mutually knowable, collective and hierarchical. The coming into being of a public for popular writing presupposes the existence of a mass culture, available in the market, and of certain recurring features within a great number of individuals: the ability to read, spare time, and an interest in what is being offered as mass cultural products.

The urban origins of popular writing are again reflected in its representation of dominant themes as for instance seen in the urban novels of Cyprian Ekwensi from Nigeria or Meja Mwangi from Kenya. In Rhodesia the colonial Literature Bureau advised the Shona and Ndebele writers that particularly the urban rural conflict was a suitable theme for literary treatment.

What Richard Mabala of the University of Dar es Salaam writes about modern Swahili popular literature in Tanzania is equally true of English language popular literature in Kenya: "Popular literature reflects and speaks to the rising urban classes. The writers themselves are of and for these classes ... [T]heir works express ... the preoccupations and contradictions of those classes." Mabala suggests that the popular writers are not simply "an urban phenomenon but in fact ... are representatives of the classes of the future" (Mabala 1990: 30). This is a different way of expressing the central point of this chapter: by placing certain important issues on the agenda in particular ways and in particular genres popular writing contributes to imagining new ways of life, and invents the language to do so. It is an element in a process which makes it possible for people "to live in the neighbourhood of their dreams" to quote Kenneth Watene, a pioneer Kenyan playwright and popular writer (Watene 1974: 86).

I wish to look at the role of popular literature in the creation of discourses of the ordinary from two perspectives. In the first case I want to treat some popular novels mainly from Kenya as data or raw material. They will be seen as a source of insight into the way meanings are created and identities are formed and discussed. In a popular novel characters inhabit and embody social dimensions like class, ethnicity, gender, and age, and negotiate them in terms of social and cultural tensions, the most important ones being perhaps those between rural/urban, male/female, and power/powerlessness. These tensions are often the central theme of the novels. The important fictional characters are types, e.g. the prostitute, the criminal, the rural wife newly arrived in the city, the big man—individual incarnations and illustrations of clusters of social configurations and problems. At the same time, the characters are realistic figures, rooted in everyday life by their language, mundane concerns, and problems in fulfilling even the most basic of needs.

From the other perspective what interests me is the creation and influence of discourses as a *process*, which means that the focus will be slightly different. Ideally the whole movement of cultural change should be followed: from the presence of the modernising cultural institutions and practices to the way they influence vocabulary and meanings in popular writing, to the reception of that literature by readers, and possible impacts. The approach I advocate is one which seeks to find discourses or discursive practices in institutions, and traces of institutional forms and social practices in discourses. An institution need not be fully fledged, but may be an institutionalising process which highlights and structures certain features within a community.[1] The written material suited to illuminate this process is seen not so much as unchangeable raw material, but rather as a part of a discursive process. In this latter case I want to take the example of a Nairobi popular magazine, and look at its way of reflecting institutions and making sense of city life in a dialogue with readers.

A different way of suggesting the overall perspective from which I work is to stress the didactic and socializing nature of popular writing—didactic from the point of view of the producers, socializing from the point of view of the recipients. Historically oral and written narratives have been important socializing agencies, closely connected to social and religious institutions. Popular narratives have continued to articulate areas of concern and contest, although now de-linked from traditional social events and institutions. In their oral form through everyday communication, heightened in debate and rumour, "Let me be a gossiper/Let me be a discusser/ That is how one learns," says the woman in a widely read narrative poem called *What Does a Man Want?* (Likimani 1974: 109). In their written forms popular narratives are available in the market and in modern institutions. The well known Onitsha market manuals are examples of this as are the novels of Grace Ogot with their traditional Luo lore, centrally placed in the school syllabus in Kenya.

Popular novels

Straightforward educational material abounds in popular writing. In *The Price of Sin*, a Kenyan novel from 1982, Ida and Macharia are romantically involved. He takes her out in his Corolla car, and they discuss the virtues of Japanese versus American cars:

---

1. See Frederiksen 1990 for a further discussion of discourse, communities and institutions.

"Japs are good at copying and improving on existing inventions," Machira tells his girl friend. "I understand that they are fifth in the world in car manufacture?" Ida says as if not sure if she was correct. "My goodness no, they are first in car manufacture, followed by the United States of America." "Sure? I thought the U.S.A. were leading in everything." "Well, they are a very great and powerful nation, but by no means the first in everything. The Japanese are leading in motor vehicle manufacture, U.S.A. second, Germany third. But considering industries as a whole, the U.S.A. leads the way, followed by West Germany, U.S.S.R. and Japan in fourth place they could easily get to the second place in a very short time." (Mwaura 1982: 37)

In this novel the topics for discussion move from the global to the African to the local. A group of friends discuss the Biafra war, and the disagreements are settled in a most peaceful and honourable way—a model of conflict resolution:

"We shall not fight over principles—you have the right to your opinion, and I have mine," Kinuthia tried to reconcile ... "Shall we vote" ... "I am for Ojwuku," Arap Chogge stated. "Me too," Lucy joined. "You see," Veronica offered her hand to Kinuthia, who shook her hand and congratulated her for winning the debate. (Mwaura 1982: 72)

The group of friends are modern, not only in being of different sexes, but also of mixed ethnicity. The novel makes a point of this, and true to its didactic thrust ethnicity becomes the subject of another brief lecture:

Arap Chogge next educated the girls on the relationship between Lumbwa, Nandi and Kalenjin as follows—"Kalenjin is a collective name for nine tribes or clans each with distinct customs, but with a lot of similarities. We understand one another when we speak although we may be unable to catch all the words spoken by a different group ... but it is generally agreed that we had a common ancestor, and therefore one common language."

The lecture becomes a discussion of the parallels between the Kalenjin identity and that constituted by the related Kikuyu, Embu and Meru peoples—GEMA (interesting in the light of recent ethnic/political violence between Kalenjin and Kikuyu in Central Province), and speeds on to debate the unity of the Empire, made up by "Vikings, Goths, Britons, English," and "by Jingo ... they danced where the sun never set" (Mwaura 1982: 66). Bits and pieces of useful knowledge and concepts from a wider world are fairly effortlessly incorporated in a fast moving story of romance and modernity.

Whereas it is unusual that ethnic tensions among Africans are put on the agenda by popular novels, conflicts between Africans and Asians are a stock in trade—maybe vicariously making space and creating language suited to debate African ethnicity. In Kenya, as in many other African countries, open debates about ethnicity were discouraged after Independence. Nation and not ethnicity was seen as the category in terms of which difference was constituted and the country's future should take shape. In Kenya there has not been a need for overt censorship on this issue because popular literature has been part of a centralised and manageable political culture, and because the nationalist project has been characterized by a high degree of consensus.

Asians were not central in the political culture of Kenya. They played an important part in pre-independence nationalist politics, but were not very visible in post-independence political life, and did not have a strong *public* voice in the political arrangements of the country. On the other hand, they were very much present in the professions, and in trade and service, and the Asian community is very visible in the social make up of modern Kenya, particularly in urban areas. Everyday conflicts and debates about power, inequality and access to resources are being fought out in the discourse of Asian-African race, class, and ethnicity.

Many popular novels take these conflicts and relations between Asians and Africans, which most commonly revolve around love and money, as their main theme. In many more relations with Asians are a sub-theme. In the universe of *Going Down River Road*, by Meja Mwangi, one of the most influential Kenyan novels, Asians are a minor irritant, the novel's real interest is relations between Africans. Asians and Africans work together on the building site of the ironically named Development House, but each go their own way during their free time:

> The four Banianis sit together away from everybody else and play cards. They rarely mix with anybody else. They bring their own lunch, eat together, then play cards in Gujarati. (Mwangi 1976: 40)

The separateness of all spheres of Asian life except the work sphere seems to arouse a good deal of resentment:

> He could not understand why he felt so sore about people who were not black ... and especially the Indians. Why did they live in separation as if they belonged to another world? Why was it that they looked so unconcerned? The

whole population could have died off and still they would have stuck to their shops. (Watene 1974: 99)

Mixing is the progressive ideal, as reflected in the titles of two novels by Mwangi Gicheru, *Across the Bridge* and *The Mixers.*

In the following conversation about powerlessness among two African mechanics in the employment of an Asian the language of nation and class is intermingled with ethnic concerns—eating habits and hygiene:

"I don't like Asians, Fred. That's Jack telling me. He hates them anyway. I also hate them. The other day, Jack told an Asian foreman at the garage that he would shave him with a screw-driver, if the foreman did not take his pink-pigment from Jack's sight."

The two friends dream of opening their own garage:

"We shall employ our own mechanics ... I cannot stand an Asian telling me when to eat or when to shit and such-like things. I am a grown-up and this is not Delhi or Bombay. This is Nakuru—Kenya!," he finishes. I agree with him. (Githae 1987)

It is striking that in most novels which take African-Asian human relations as their central theme the issue is dealt with in what might be called a progressive or modern way. From initial hostility and portrayal of particularly the older generations as being die-hard ethnic individuals, the resolution negotiated by mainly young people implies that persons should be evaluated on the basis of their personal merit—not cast as ethnic or racial stereotypes. Understanding other cultures is seen as the essence of being modern. In *Day after Tomorrow* written by a Ugandan Asian, Bahadur Tejani, empathy is most important. The young African woman, who is in love with an Indian, is described in this way: "Nanziri was a modern woman.... She possessed the powers of imagination and sympathy which allow modern people to project themselves into the minds of other people, other cultures" (Tejani 1971: 86).

I Will Be Your Substitute by a woman writer, Pat Wambui Ngurukie, plays out another popular fantasy: of African entry into the Asian trade and economy via a love relationship. A young African woman, Nyokabi, falls in love with an Asian, and ends up by marrying him in a traditional Asian costume. The story revolves around the activities of a River Road fashion shop, Mona Boutique, owned by Indians, in which Nyokabi, now Carol, makes herself

indispensible, partly by recognising the culture of the customers—
for instance being able to greet a Luo woman in her own language.
Empathy is again essential.

In *Untouchable* by Kenya's most popular writer, David Maillu, the
young couple are an African man, Moses, and an Indian woman,
symbolically named Kenindia. They plan to start a "club for race relations," or a magazine: "The written word can be very powerful in
influencing people," Moses tells his girl friend, and she "had picked
up quite a number of university words for him, such as *symbiosis,
gastronomy, ecology, dichotomy,* and *vis-a-vis*" (Maillu 1987: 16, 14). If
there is any magic present in this writing it is the belief in words
having the effect of bringing about a new and modern reality. In a
bar scene from Kenneth Watene's novel, *Sunset on the Manyatta,* the
hero is being overwhelmed by a prostitute "who smothered him
with kisses, calling him every single word she had read," and he re-
sponds in kind and "addressed this woman with the finest words
dug out of paper-back vocabulary" (Watene 1974: 66).

The young hero of the Congolese novelist Emmanuel Dongala's
first novel about the early generation of African freedom fighters believes in the magic of words, and especially in the power of French
words—the language of education:

> He loved to scan French words, to say them out loudly, even if their ordering
> made no sense; he found a magic quality in those words, as if something was
> hidden in them, behind the syllables, some kind of force which would be open
> to him if he could master them. (Dongala 1973: 189)

The power of words is explained in this way:

> ... in this Africa ... deeds and words are but two sides of the same thing; ... a
> man is judged as severely for an opinion which he expresses as for an act which
> he commits.... Here a word was not free as in the West—if it were how was it
> possible to have built a whole civilisation without writing? (Dongala 1973: 125)

It is no accident that the most prevalent state of mind of the fictional
characters in a cross section of popular novels is confusion. The distance between the imagined good life and the experienced reality is
too great. It may be bridged, imaginatively, at the level of language.
This happens in political, bureaucratic and popular culture discourses. But the social and economic processes sustaining the various discourses are disjointed and out of phase. In Meja Mwangi's recent *Striving for the Wind* the alcoholic hero Juda's faithful compan-

ion, a dog, is called Confucias (*sic!*) the Thinker. The naming reflects the void at the centre of the rural community which is depicted in the novel—a potentially affluent community of farmers in Central Kenya. Only the Big Man, Baba Pesa, acts with the energy necessary to perpetuate his own wealth, but does so with a ruthlessness and lack of standards which finally erode the authority and communication infrastructure which even he has to rely on: "In the Tajiri Bar, Baba Pesa was in the process of making worms of everyone, turning them into creatures so tiny you couldn't see most of them crouched behind the beer bottles he had bought for them" (Mwangi 1990: 64).

The market day is the "weekly madness"—no economic activities take place, only drunken turmoil of disoriented people, "the market square milled with people, a seething, aimless throng in desperate need of a leader" (Mwangi 1990: 75). On this particular day a rain ceremony is supposed to take place, but nobody is in charge. The village madman, Ndege, is the one who, as madmen will, diagnoses "the lack of any comprehensible pattern to the event of the day," and he decides to add to the "world-turned-upside-down" quality of the whole thing by stripping naked and running through the square, "to the amusement of the bored herdsboys and to the extreme embarassment of the venerable rain-makers" (Mwangi: 1990: 77).

When Baba Pesa, a potential leader arrives, he adds to the confusion by having decorated his tractor so that it looks "more like a witch-doctor's matatu than a farm truck," and by wearing an unprincipled collection of traditional items of clothing:

> He had on him, noted the old ..., a chief's colobus monkey head-dress, a circumcisor's sykes monkey cloak, a witch-doctor's hyena-skin apron, an elder's black and white cowhide robe ... and even, much to the embarrassment of those who recognized it, a woman's traditional loin skin called *muthuru*, a much venerated dress that only a woman's husband was allowed to even touch. (Mwangi 1990: 77-78)

His son Juda describes his parading of the "entire dress culture of his people" as "this chaotic return to the roots," a return which Juda himself equally ineffectually advocates after having taken useless university degrees in Nairobi. In this novel the theme of power and powerlessness is played through in a rural setting, but by an urban writer, who knows more about the disillusion of failed male academics such as Juda, than about aspirations and feelings of his female partner, the young Margaret, who becomes impregnated by Baba Pesa. She suffers the standard fate of women characters whom the male author cannot inspire to live: she dies giving birth to male twins.

If the novels themselves are also sometimes confused or even chaotic they represent a world where things are out of joint. In many novels the narrative structure is picaresque. Keeping the protagonist from falling to pieces takes so much of the narrative energy that none is left for a coherent plot. One might argue that a plot presupposes a world in which things make sense and fit together—the very opposite of the social milieux represented in popular novels. On the other hand a neat and tidy plot might also be said to represent the pleasing ideal of an orderly life, and in fact most novels have orderly endings, doling out rewards and punishments to the characters according to their deserts.

A popular magazine

In order to highlight the communicative process of popular writing I now wish to turn to a popular magazine, *Joe*, which came out in Nairobi in the 1970s.[2]

Why is a popular magazine interesting? From the point of view of communicative process a magazine is able to pick up new social and cultural currents quickly, and its format allows readers to influence it to a high degree. From the point of view of form and content it is characterised by a rich and varied everyday discourse—richer, perhaps, than the one we find in conventional genres such as fiction, painting and music.

A magazine is made up of a mixture of genres and formats. Writing includes editorials, feature articles, pastiches, spoofs, reviews, competitions, short stories, advertisements, jokes, genuine and faked letters from readers. The graphic work also appears in many sub-genres, the full-page satirical drawing, cartoons, comic strips with speech bubbles, illustrated narratives and jokes, and once again advertisements. The magazine circles around its chosen theme, throws light on it from various angles, with varying degrees of seriousness, in words and pictures, advising readers and making fun of them. The whole thing represents a variety in form which throws a multi-faceted light on the fairly limited number of issues. It mimicks

---

2. For a fuller treatment of *Joe* see Frederiksen 1991 b.

everyday life—also a mixture of impulses and modes of communication—and contributes to the creation of a discursive context in
which everyday concerns make sense and are made to seem significant.

Joe was a mouthpiece for the experience and aspirations of the
new African middle and lower middle classes in Kenya in which issues of concern might be discussed,[3] a socializing agent, educating
people in how to be modern and urban, and a contribution to a fairly
democratic public sphere in which political issues could be voiced
and discussed.

The magazine came out fairly regularly once or twice a month in
Nairobi between 1973 and 1979. It took its name from a popular
character in a satirical column in the *Daily Nation*—"With a Light
Touch"—written by Hilary Ng'weno and illustrated by Terry Hirst.
Its circulation fluctuated between ten and thirty thousand copies.
Every number had thirty-two pages, and started out costing one
shilling, rising to five towards the end. Until 1975 the staff were
Hilary Ng'weno and Terry Hirst. At the beginning Hirst was mainly
responsible for the artwork. In the beginning of 1975 Hilary
Ng'weno left the magazine, and Terry Hirst became the new editor
with Nereas Gicoru as the business manager. This construction was
kept through the years with the addition of some younger editors
and contributors.

The notion of Joe, the common man, "a survivor who has to laugh
to keep from crying" (Terry Hirst) was the pivot around which the
concerns of the magazine revolved. He was immediately recogniz-
able by Kenyans as a type—a street wise frequenter of bars, ever
ready with gossip and rumours, pragmatic, with his eye on the main
chance, but basically good-natured. Drawn by Terry Hirst, Joe was
on the front cover of most of the magazines, now dressed up as a
tourist Masai, now on the operating table in an issue dealing with
the medical services, now in a derelict and empty shop, reading
"How to Succeed in Business" in one dealing with the small businessman. He was portrayed as always slightly disreputable, balding
with a stubbled chin, and accompanied by his dog.

He appeared in every issue in a feature called "My Friend Joe,"
talking to friends in the bar: "Wait a minute. Drinking is the most
African thing God ever created after creating the African race. Look

---

3. On the concept "issue of concern" see Frederiksen 1991 a.

around you. What do you see? Drunks. African drunks. I tell you that's the most African thing on this earth, drinking" (November 1974). His was the voice of *Joe*, relaxed but insistent, down to earth and inviting dialogue. The magazine encouraged conversation, it wanted readers to write to the magazine, to give editorial suggestions. Joe himself solicited letters from the readers, "Why don't you drop me a letter expressing your feelings about things—even about me? I might print it—and then I might not. Joe."

Readers were invited to take part in the making of *Joe* in several ways. Every issue carried two pages of jokes with illustrations—"Joe's Bar Jokes"—for which they were asked to send in their best jokes and paid ten shillings for each one published. According to Terry Hirst there was a massive response, people making up jokes themselves, or picking them up from old copies of *Reader's Digest* (Lindfors 1979: 89). *Joe* also ran various competitions such as, "How many titles of African novels do you know?," or "Con-Men Observed: In 250 words readers are asked to describe a 'con-trick' of their own." Two features embodied the dialogic ideal which was central to the magazine. One was called "Ask a Stupid Question" and would show Joe being asked a naive question by some up country person or by a tourist. He would then provide some "snappy answers." The other was "Reporter Roving Mike," interviewing a selection of "typical" Kenyans on the theme of the issue, all invented and drawn by Terry Hirst.

Most numbers of *Joe* contained quick exchanges with readers, as well as humorous responses to small and big events in the everyday life of Kenyans. In one issue it announced the granting of the OBE (Only Bosses Eat) award to a columnist from *The Nation*, Virginia, "who can't imagine why food kiosks keep springing up in the Industrial Area after the Keep the City Clean cleaners have pulled them down."

One of the magazine's chief attractions was undoubtedly the amount of high quality graphic work which was spread liberally all throughout the magazine. All short stories and many feature articles were illustrated, usually in very eye-catching styles. Comic strips played a prominent role, many of them reflecting the urban slant of the magazine, showing the pleasures and the dangers of big city life. The most striking and original comic strip, or rather drawn narrative, was "Gitau E. on City Life." It consisted of six or seven carefully

Two *Joe* covers
One depicting transportation (15 January 1976), the other the medical services (29 January 1976).

filled out frames, depicting incidents of the city—of what happens when the ignorant rural person comes to Nairobi. It was drawn by the well established artist Edward Gitau, known as the creator of *Kalulu* in *Taifa Leo*.

Each issue of *Joe* had a particular theme which coloured almost every written and graphic item in the magazine. The themes were social rather than political, and most had to do with modern institutions or clusters of social problems. The problems were mainly seen as quality of life problems—there were not many attempts to look into the underlying causes of the particular problems. Five numbers dealt with women and gender relations. The theme of the first— "Women's War: Uganda vs. Kenya"—was the reaction of Kenyan women (and men) to the influx of Ugandan women in the wake of the civil war. Many of the women were prostitutes, or were seen as such. The general trend of the (humorous) articles was that the Ugandan women were in fact welcome to take over the Kenyan men, who were "either too drunk or too stupid." Marriage was one of the changing institutions to be taken up by *Joe* and dealt with fairly thoroughly. Others were the Medical Services, the Civil Service, and the Church. Three *Joe* issues dealt with youth, education and employment. Other issues, such as "Rolling Joe" on rock and pop music, were also primarily directed at a youth audience.

Traffic was dealt with in "Transports of Delight." The informal institution of the Matatu figures prominently in this issue. In "With a Little Help from a Matatu" Sam Kahiga, a regular contributor of fiction and satirical colums, described the daily experience of getting to work in Nairobi: "From around the corner, like a little busy bee comes a matatu rushing into the bus stage at a hundred KPH. A little happy road pirate with worn-out brakes, tyres as smooth as oranges, a 1973 road licence, a forged log book, a driver with three hangovers piled up together, and a conductor who was once nuts. It rushes in, its radiator boiling with enthusiasm. Its motto: TRUST IN GOD."

A page of cartoons, "Close to the Tarmac," illustrated traffic-related incidents in the life of Kenyans, and the stupid question of "Ask a Stupid Question" for this issue was, "Do Busses Stop Here?," some of the snappy answers, "Possibly, if you are brave enough to lie down in the road!," "I'm not sure, I've only been waiting here for three hours!"

Housing was the theme of two issues. In "The Housing Scene" Joe is worried that he "may have to move out to Mathare Valley," and is warned by his friend: "Once in a while the City Council will come tearing down your home.... And there will be the chang'aa drinkers and the criminal types ... Man, Mathare Valley is just not the place for you, Joe" (in "My Friend Joe"). The June 1976 issue on "Habitat and Shelter" coincided with a conference on that theme at the Kenyatta Conference Centre. An article points out that while from a great height slum houses are an eye-sore, for the people who have built them and live in them they represent "a tremendous investment in terms of labour and capital."

In "The Small Businessman" (March 1976), which appeared at the time of the ILO interest in the Kenya informal sector, a business section, "Business *Joe*," reported on the fluctuations at the Mathare Stock Exchange, and the merger between Pius Mbitiri, waste paper collector, and the "doyen of the recycled bottle trade, Mama Njeri." The number also contained down-to-earth advice, both in a serious and jocular manner, on how to set up a business—"avoid middlemen!" Two issues on witchcraft and on con-men were related, not only because many *ngangas* were con-men, but also because they both explicitly dealt with anxieties and ambitions of modernity, particularly in its urban version.

All fiction carried by *Joe* was local: written by Kenyans or Ugandans—in the 1970s Kenya and Uganda was very much one literary millieu—set locally and dealing with local issues: money, alcohol, unemployment, corruption, prostitution, unfaithfulness. Bars were a favourite location, and men were protagonists in most stories although women were present, but mostly as a problem. Like other magazines from the same period, *Joe* carried an original short story in every issue.[4] Some were by writers who were already well known, or have since become so. Ngugi wa Thiong'o's "A Mercedes Funeral" appeared in two parts in early numbers, David Maillu wrote stories for the magazine, and it brought three short stories by Meja Mwangi: "Like Manna from Heaven," "No Credit, Terms Strictly Cash," and "Incident in the Park."

The stories by Mwangi are typical of the style and themes of of the *Joe* short story. The opening lines of "Like Manna from Heaven" (November 1974) run like this: "The evening blows cold, rather

---

4. *Drum* magazine featured short stories regularly. On the large body of Swahili fiction, published in newspapers—*Taifa Weekly, Baraza* and *Fahari* —see Lepine 1990.

windy. Ben pulls his coat tight round his chest as he makes his way through the parking lot." Ben is moneyless, looking for a job and meets a prospective employer in a bar. They quarrel over the bill and Ben's job chances evaporate in a drunken brawl.

Some writers were influenced by the tough guy style of American thrillers of the James Hadley Chase type, although they kept an authentic, or perhaps mock-Kenyan flavour, "Holy Ngai!" instead of "Holy God!" Or this description from a story called "Pubic Relations" by Johnie Olimba (April 29 1976): Larry Nyita is walking down Kimathi Street "in flat heeled shoes. The highly polished tops belied the worn out soles, which he replaced daily with layers of cardboard." He is down on his luck and meets Nick, his old school mate, "in swinging bellbottom black and white check trousers ... a black silk shirt that clung to him like a rainy day in the Aberdares, and Man ... those platform boots, black with silver tasselled zippers."

Life style, or quality of life, was of the utmost importance in these stories. When down-and-out Larry comes to see Nick at his home in the evening, this is the setting: "centre of town, modern bedsitter, slick and classy, shining bathroom all white tiles, flush choo, big veranda overlooking the main drag, from where you can see it all ... T.V., Radio and Record player all built into the wall." Nick is there "stretched out on his bed-cum-sofa," and with him his secretary, "the cutest chick." The writing carries the reader out of this world into the realm of fantasy in spite of the faithfully rendered specifications of interior design. Larry is set up as a successful public relations man, hence the word play of the title. The most important part of the setting up is again style—the new outfit he gets for himself. He discards his old life in his "four-in-a-bed cube," and his old clothes on which "even the stains had stains." Fantasy here, as in most of the *Joe* stories, reflected urban preoccupations and did not detract from the basic realism of the narratives.

"Don't Trust the Playgirls who Live in the Cities" is the title of one of the Swahili stories from *Baraza* listed by Lepine in his examination of Swahili newspaper fiction; another is called "Love Affairs with Playgirls Poison for Executives."[5] These stories and countless more in the same vein, indicate the preoccupation with modern marriage, prostitution and the unequal situation of men and women

---

5. *Usiamini Vipusa Waishio Mijini*, by F. Mubezi and *Mapenzi ya Vidosho Sumu kwa Wenye Madaraka* by F. Dumila.

in the cities, which is a central theme in popular culture, and also present in *Joe*.

The five stories in the magazine about marriage also dealt with infidelity. In "The Elected Ones" by David Maillu (August 1973) the husband is a successful executive, fairly happily married: "When he married her she was slim; now she was nicely round. But now things had, sort of, changed. Sleeping with her was like one of his duties. After it was over he hardly thought about it. He began thinking about money, politics, new girls and himself." In "A Day in your Life" by Njuguna Wainaina (November 1973) the theme is similar, but there are two points of view. Both the husband, the executive, and his wife have affairs—he contracts veneral disease, she becomes pregnant by her lover. In modern marriages both the partners have a problem.

In a letter from a reader Meja Mwangi's short story, "Manna from Heaven" is praised: "*Joe* is really proving to be a stimulus to creativity in East Africa and will prove to have a lasting place in the history of African communicators." But the letter writer has a suggestion: "What about some stories like "Manna from Heaven" where the central character is a woman?" In a review of David Maillu's *After 4.30* (January 1975) the woman question is again linked with literature: "The women represented in the book-length poem are voices of disillusion in and criticism of married life in a modern African city." According to the review "square social commentary on the nascent urban communities in East Africa" is finding a voice in literature, and a forum in *Joe*. The review goes on to specify that Maillu's book deals with "urban lifestyles," particularly to do with the uneven development of the two sexes.[6]

Conclusion

I wish to return to the claims which I made for *Joe*, and to see whether in fact the magazine lived up to them. I suggested that *Joe* served as a mouthpiece for aspirations and issues of concern to middle and lower middle-class Africans, that it functioned as a socializ-

---

6. One short story in *Baraza* by T. Pella was called, "I Can't Get Married to You Because You're Uneducated" (*Siwezi Kuolewa Nawe Kwani Huna Eliu*) (Lepine 1976).

ing agent, educating people in how to be modern and urban, and that it constituted a fairly open and democratic public sphere, perhaps one of the few which was available in Kenya.

The magazine was written and drawn by Africans, and advertisements were also directed at the African majority of the population. The readers who wrote letters and sent in jokes were almost all African, judging from their names. This is of particular interest only if the issues and themes reflected in the magazine were of central concern to emerging and modernizing sections of the African population. This can be confirmed or not, as the case may be, by interviewing readers, by consulting newspapers, novels and popular music of the same period, and by the findings of urban ethnography. It is likely, however, that themes like housing, transport, marriage and sex, jobs and education, witchcraft, and the law constitute areas of concern.[7] The magazine, dealing with variations on these themes, sold well. It is fair to say that *Joe* magazine functioned as a mouthpiece for issues of concern to the African middle and lower middle classes.

I claim that there was in *Joe* a preoccupation with *urban* life, not modern life in general, but its versions in cities. The evidence for this takes several forms. First of all the language, including the coining of new expressions, was repeated until they have become familiar: "On the tarmac," "Urban Nomads," "A City Girl's View," "On City Life," "A Nairobi Tale." The settings and topics of the short stories reflect the urban preoccupation of writers for the magazine, as do the themes around which each issue was organised. Finally the magazine covered the important cultural events of the city, particularly theatre and music.

The knitting together of language and themes was brought about by the particular didactic stance of *Joe*. Part of its make-up was a discreet didacticism, a will to educate—hence the claim for *Joe* as a conscious socializing agent. In spite of the magazine's irreverence, it has a flavour of the class room, for instance in straightforward features like "Facts from History," but also in unlikely places, e.g. the crossword puzzle and "Gitau E. On City Life"—*Lehrstücke* of the slums.

---

7. Some writers were very conscious of what might interest the reading public. David Maillu states that he has systematically studied the "psychology of the African reader and the African storyteller." In an interview with Bernth Lindfors he tells that he "tried to find out what they liked talking about and hearing" (Lindfors 1979: 86).

The last claim, that *Joe* functioned as a fairly open and democratic public sphere, is more problematic. In the first place it only worked as such for the limited part of the population who spoke English and spent money on the magazine. If the average number of copies published was twenty thousand, and each was read by about ten people, which was *Joe*'s own estimate, that public sphere was relevant to about two hundred thousand people in Kenya plus their immediate communities. But they, of course, were the modern elite and set trends.

Magazines in Kenya are more visible than novels. They are sold from the pavement, read on street corners, and circulate widely. They are also more sharply supervised by the authorities: editors and contributors are frequently taken in for questioning. *Joe* was dependent on advertising, and it was a humorous magazine. So for several reasons it was even more wary of taking up controversial political issues than were popular novels. Representations of ethnic and racial tensions were absent from its pages. Whites and Asians might not have existed in Kenya, judging from the magazine. And the well known corruption of Kenyatta's last years, which coincided with the period in which *Joe* came out, was only hinted at.

The direction of communication, particularly on controversial issues, was naturally mostly from the magazine to the readers. In early numbers of *Joe* some of the Letters to the Editor dealt with serious issues, but as time went on contributions from readers became increasingly light-hearted. A conversational ease was the ideal. In its *form* the magazine encouraged the habit of discussion and dialogue, but when it came to bringing serious issues into play in that discussion, it was less successful.

If *Joe* lived up to the claims to the extent I have suggested, it follows that it is of interest in an examination of the role of popular writing in shaping everyday life in Nairobi in the period it covers. It was part of a communication process. It responded quickly to fashions and innovations, made institutions familiar, and contributed to dismantling barriers which were irrelevant to modern city life.

I have suggested a complex of meanings and practices which are tightly linked and interdependent in the material discussed: urbanism, education, empathy, multi-linguism, modernity, affluence, and maybe youth. The ideal individual who can live out his or her dreams is an embodiment of a complex of attributes. Together articulations from within the complex shape the discourse of the ordinary, or of the good life. The tension and dreariness in a number of popular narratives come from the characters' falling short of experiencing that life. They master the discourse, but language is after all not magical—naming something does not bring it about. A discourse of the kind I have tried to characterise does, however, give people the possibility of "living in the neighbourhood of their dreams." That, perhaps, is the appeal of popular writing.

Bibliography

Barber, Karin. 1987. "Popular Arts in Africa." *African Studies Review* 30.3: 1–78.
Bardolph, Jacqueline. 1983. "Naissance d'une littérature populaire à Nairobi." *L'Afrique Litteraire* 67: 160–74.
Dawood, Yusuf K. 1983. *The Price of Living*. Nairobi: Longman.
Dawood, Yusuf K. 1991. *Water under the Bridge*. Nairobi: Longman.
Dongala, Emmanuel. 1973. *Un fusil dans la main, un poème dans la poche*. Paris: Albin Michel.
Frederiksen, Bodil Folke. 1990. "Discourse, Communities and Institutions." In *Selected Approaches to the Study of Institutions in Development*, ed. John Martinussen. International Development Studies, Occasional Paper no. 1. Roskilde: 69–74.
Frederiksen, Bodil Folke. 1991a. "City Life and City Texts. Popular Knowledge and Articulation in the Slums of Nairobi." In *Culture and Development in Southern Africa*, ed. Preben Kaarsholm. London: James Currey: 227–37.
Frederiksen, Bodil Folke. 1991b. "*Joe*, the Sweetest Reading in Africa: Documentation and discussion of a popular magazine in Kenya." *African Languages and Cultures* 4.2: 135–55.
Gicheru, Mwangi. 1979. *Across the Bridge*. Nairobi: Longman.
Gicheru, Mwangi. 1991. *The Mixers*. Nairobi: Longman.
Githae, Charles K. 1987. *A Worm in the Head*. Nairobi: Heinemann.
Lepine, Richard Marshall. 1990. "Swahili Newspaper Fiction in Kenya: The Stories of James I. Mwagojo." Ph. D. dissertation. University of Wisconsin-Madison.
Likimani, Muthoni. 1974. *What does a Man Want?* Nairobi: Kenya Literature Bureau.
Lindfors, Bernth. 1979. "Interview with David Maillu." *The African Book Publishing Record* 5.2: 85–88.
Mabala, Richard. 1990. "Popular Literature in Tanzania." Paper presented to AATOLL, Botswana.
Maillu, David. 1987. *Untouchable*. Nairobi: David Maillu Publishing.
Mwangi, Meja. 1976. *Going down River Road*. London: Heinemann.
Mwangi, Meja. 1990. *Striving for the Wind*. Nairobi: Heinemann.
Mwaura, J.M. 1982. *The Price of Sin*. Nairobi: Kenya Literature Bureau.
Ngurukie, Pat Wambui. 1984. *I will be your Substitute*. Nairobi: Kenya Literature Bureau.
Tejani, Bahadur. 1971. *Day after Tomorrow*. Nairobi: East African Literature Bureau.
Watene, Kenneth. 1974. *Sunset on the Manyatta*. Nairobi: East African Publishing House.

Oppression and Liberation of Kenyan Women: On Orature and Modern Women's Literature

Ingrid Björkman

There is a tendency to regard the traditional and the modern society of Africa as two clearly defined models where the traditional form has been succeeded at a certain stage by a modern. Both forms have existed, however, side by side for a long time, or rather interwined with each other. Although urban Africa is in many ways modern, it is also to a great extent traditional. Orature plays an important role in mediating information and transferring norms and values.

What is, then, "orature"? It is a broad phenomenon that includes not only oral literature in its various forms, such as narratives, proverbs, riddles and songs; it also involves the performance of oral literature and the interaction of the storyteller and the audience. African orature is verbal, dramatized and performed art.

The storyteller's skill is measured by her impact on the audience. Talented storytellers are not only sensitive to the moods of the audience. They are also skilful actors who identify with the characters they perform, whether these are human beings, animals or monsters.

The active participation of the audience is characteristic of African orature. The footlights—a feature which is implied by the notion "audience"—do not exist in this context. The audience and the storyteller influence each other mutually, they co-operate and control the performance. Through questions and calls the storyteller invites the listeners to participate. But even without her calls the listeners will break into the performance with questions, exclamations, additions, emphatic repetitions of her words, and with all kinds of comments. This is expected, because the performing role of the audience is part and parcel of collective drama.

In this chapter, I will focus on a specific category of the orature: the tales which make up the most common form of the narratives. The tales picture well-known conditions, and they always convey a moral message. Even if the entertaining function of orature should not be underrated, its didactic purpose is clear, and the listeners always know that the tale will teach them something useful and important. Thus, after having finished her story the storyteller usually asks: "What can we now learn from this story?" And a vivid discussion among the audience follows.

The tales demonstrate the kind of life that was right according to the norm system of society. They also present strategies and guides to help the individuals to live this life. Through warning examples they show how things go badly for those who do not obey conventional norms, and through positive role models, how those who obey the norms gain success. As will be shown below, it may, however, happen that a disobedient woman is successful.

The survival of the community, which was a prerequisite for the survival of the individual, was regarded the ultimate purpose of all efforts. The individual was, therefore, first of all identified as a member of the social collective. The members of society had to keep together in order to survive the struggle against nature and the wars against other societies. The tales encourage, therefore, concord and unity within the family, the village, the clan. They tell their listeners how things go badly for those who cause disruption within the community—for example jealous co-wives and evil stepmothers—and also for those who abandon their own group—for example young girls who marry strangers.

Storytelling is not confined to reproduction. Nor is it "frozen" like the printed word which becomes fixed to paper. It allows for self-expression, renewal, innovation, and creativity. In every performance, elements are consciously or unconsciously changed, added or removed. The content of the tale is adapted to the audience, the situation, the specific context. "The messages," J. Vansina writes, "are significant to members of the communities in which they are told. Otherwise they would not be communicated at all."[1] Old stories are changed in order to illustrate the life style of modern times. Thus, the storytellers are regarded as true creators of literary art. And all orature is, in Ruth Finnegan's words, "in one sense a unique literary work—the work rendered on one occasion."[2]

The storytellers were, and are, mostly women. Since every rendering also includes interpretation which is controlled by the performer's personality and background experiences, changes in the ora-

---

1. J. Vansina, *Oral Tradition as History* (Nairobi: Heinemann, 1976) 94.
2. R. Finnegan, *Oral Literature in Africa* (Oxford: Clarendon, 1975) 9.

ture, as symptoms, arouse a specific interest from a women's per-spective. How much of the tale was changed during the storytelling? For what reasons were the changes carried out? To what extent did the storyteller act as a mouthpiece of her society? What impact on the tale had her own creative individuality?

These issues are closely connected with the question of what ora-ture tells us about the view of women held by traditional society. This society was patriarchal but its values were mediated mainly by women. How authentically—and for what reasons—did the story-tellers convey a patriarchal view of women? Are there any signs in the tales of women's emancipation?

Research into African orature—for example by the Kenyan re-searcher Mwikali Kieti—demonstrates that the image of women in the orature is contradictory.[3] African orature gives clear evidence of the woman's inferior status. Most tales urge their audience to obey societal norms, norms that purport to preserve and guard the existant social structure. These norms are oppressive to women; they grant them few rights and impose on them duties instead. Woman thus belongs to man.

On the other hand, African orature also presents images of strong, independent women. There are liberating tales which show how a woman's objections to the oppressive norms of the society lead to a radical and positive change of the whole society. Such a tale is the Kikuyu tale "Wacu and the Eagle," from Mount Kenya, which tells us how, as a result of a young girl's revolt against a the patriarchal tradi-tion, women were allowed to eat meat which had earlier been re-served exclusively for men. It is hard to believe that such a dynamic and liberating view of women represented the official view of society. It is more likely to be the expression of an independent and liberated woman's creative individuality, a call to break the norms of patriar-chal society.

African women writers regard themselves as "the people's teach-ers." They often emphasize their dependence on indigenous orature in terms of both the content and the form of their writing. In this con-text, the relationship between the storyteller's creative individuality and her function as a mouthpiece of society gains a wider relevance.

---

3. Mwikali Kieti is the author of *Barking, You'll Be Eaten. The Wisdom of Kamba Oral Literature* (Nairobi: Phoenix Publishers, 1990). The contradictory image of woman in African orature was demonstrated by Kieti in her lecture "From Orature to Modern Women's Literature in Kenya," at Gothenburg University, 9 March 1991.

Some women writers give prominence to the storyteller's norm-guarding function, and it is interesting to see how these writers also act themselves as norm-guarders.

The Egyptian writer Nawal el Saadawi calls the norm-guarding women writers "traditional." The traditional writers safeguard the "status quo" and are loyal to the patriarchal class system from which they benefit.

> Some women writers are *traditional*. Some women writers allow themselves to step back and forget their true selves, their reality. They practise what men practice, use their weapons to compete with them, to achieve what they refer to as glory, fame, success, and *high positions in the government*, newspapers, media, institutions and ministries of cultures, and all the other dazzling terms that blur their vision and blind their eyes to their own reality and to their creative striving towards justice, freedom and truth. If a woman slides down into the quagmire, she is assimilated by the patriarchal class system and becomes part of it. She loses her creativity even though she may continue to write.[4]

Grace Ogot, the Kenyan writer, does not only entertain a close relationship with the oral tradition, but is also a clear-cut representative of a norm-guarding woman writer. Several of Grace Ogot's stories are actually adaptations of tales she were told by her grandmother, who was a famous storyteller. Ogot is Kenya's most read woman writer and her books are included in syllabuses all over the country. She is also a successful politician: she is one of the two women members of parliament in Kenya and is Deputy Minister for Culture and Social Services. Thus she is one of those responsible for Kenyan women's development.

Her story "Elizabeth" is about a young secretary in Nairobi who will be married as soon as her fiancé returns from his studies in the United States.[5] To avoid the sexual harrassment of her bosses, Elizabeth often has to change jobs. When she finally gets a boss whom she trusts, she is raped by him. She recalls her grandmother's words: "When a mature girl plays with boys and becomes pregnant out of wedlock, she destroys herself and eventually the whole family." Discovering that she is pregnant, Elizabeth commits suicide.

Encouraged by Alan Dundes' suggestion in his Introduction to Vladimir Propp's *Morphology of the Folktale*, that Propp's analysis

---

4. N. el Saadawi, "Why so few women write," paper presented at the 1985 Writers' Workshop, Harare (mimeo).
5. The story is published in Grace Ogot, *Land Without Thunder* (Nairobi: East African Publishing House, 1968) 189–204.

might be applicable to non-Indo-European folktales and useful in examining the structure of literary forms, such as plays and novels, I have applied the syntagmatic structural method presented by Propp to my reading of "Elizabeth."[6] I then found that this story, which is laid in a modern urban setting and deals with a modern social problem, was structured like a traditional tale. Furthermore, when combining structural analysis with an analysis of the tale as a "discourse," taking into account the socio-cultural context and, in particular, the social problems, I found that the message of the story could be interpreted as a variation of the theme of "the lost girl"—a common theme in traditional Kenyan tales.

The "discourse" perspective includes the whole process of producing, interpreting and reproducing texts. It presupposes not only the text as a formal structure, but also the reflexions of a specific historic socio-cultural reality and its ideology. Since social relationships operate between the givers and receivers of literature, such relationships are embedded on the communication levels of the "discourse." A literary "discourse" is, therefore, not only an ideological product but also an instrument for ideology.

The category of tales to which "Elizabeth" is related is that of the monster tales. Many of these tales demonstrate the devastating consequences for young girls when attracted to strangers. The strangers later prove to be man-eating beasts or ogres (cannibalistic monsters). One such tale from the Rift Valley Province in Kenya is simply called "Monster."[7] It is about a girl who is not wary enough and accepts an invitation to stay overnight in a "friendly" stranger's house. The man is a monster that the poor girl has to marry, not to be eaten by him. She has a son and a daughter by him, of whom the daughter is a human being like herself and the son a monster who, when hungry, cuts pieces off his mother's body and eats them. Finally, with the help of a

---

6. V. Propp, *Morphology of the Folktale* (Austin: University of Texas Press, 1979). In the "syntagmatic" structural analysis "the structure of a folkloristic text is described following the chronological order of the linear sequence of elements in the text as reported from an informant." The other type of structural analysis in folklore is "paradigmatic" and "seeks to describe the pattern which allegedly underlies the folkloristic text." See A. Dundes' "Introduction to the Second Edition" of Propp's *Morphology*, 1979.

7. The tale is published in A. Odaga, *Yesterday's Today* (Kisumu: Lake Publishers and Enterprises, 1984) 29–32.

talking crow, the mother and her daughter are rescued by the mother's relatives.

According to Propp's syntagmatic method a tale can be analyzed according to the functions of its *dramatis personae*. These functions are the elements of which the tale is built. They are stable and constant and independent of the persons who perform them. The number of functions is limited to 31 and the number of characters is limited to seven constant roles. All tales, of course, do not contain all the functions and all the roles.

Adopting this syntagmatic method the structure of the tale "Monster" can be analyzed as follows: (the specific forms of the functions in the tale occur within brackets—after the Proppian denominations)

1. *Absentation*. (The girl and her friends leave home)
2. *Trickery*. (The girls are invited to a friendly stranger's house)
3. *Interdiction*. (The friends ask the girl to leave the stranger's house)
4. *Violation*. (The girl refuses to obey her friends)
5. *Reconnaissance*. (The stranger/monster scolds the hiding girl)
6. *Delivery*. (The girl cries and is discovered)
7. *Complicity*. (The girl agrees to marriage)
8. *Villainy*. (The girl/wife is permanently locked in. Her breast is cut off and eaten by her monster-son)
9. *Provision or reception of a magical agent*. (A talking crow delivers a message from the wife to her relatives)
10. *Initial misfortune is abolished*. (The wife and her daughter are freed by relatives)
11. *Punishment*. (The monsters are killed)

A syntagmatic analysis of "Elizabeth" gives the following result:

1. *Absentation*. (E.'s fiancé is in the United States/E. has left her family to work in Nairobi)
2. *Interdiction*. (The grandmother's warning)
3. *Violation*. (E. confides in her new boss and neglects to be cautious)
4. *Trickery*. (The boss invites E. to share his lunch)
5. *Complicity*. (E. accepts the invitation)
6. *Reconnaissance*. (The boss questions E. about her fiancé)

7. *Delivery.* (E. informs the boss that she will not be married within the next two years)
8. *Villainy.* (E. is raped by the boss)

Comparing the results one finds that, with two exceptions, the structures of the texts are identical. The first difference concerns the order of the functions. "Trickery," which in the tale is number 2, is in the story number 4. "Complicity," which in the tale is number 7, is in the story number 5. According to Propp the order of the functions is always the same. However, Denise Paulme in her research into African folklore, in which she demonstrates the cross-cultural validity of parts of Propp's *Morphology,* shows that the functions do not always have to follow the same order.[8]

The second difference is that the story ends in "villainy," which leads to the girl's death, while in the tale harmonic order is restored by "villainy," and followed by "provision of a magical agent," "liquidation of misfortune" and "punishment." Why does Ogot's story deviate from the norm of the tales, according to which the good should be rewarded and the evil get their legitimate punishment? I would like to connect the issue of the deviation of the story from normal tale structure with the issue of its connection with the category of monster tales.

Considering the decidedly oral character of today's Kenyan society, the relationship of the story to traditional orature, both structurally and content-wise, probably strengthens the impact of its message. This is the kind of literature Kenyans are used to. They recognize the structure, the characters, the issue and the message, and they know the rules and modes of interpretation. But not only the relationship of the story to the tales, but also its deviation from the conventional ending in the tales, is probably an expression of the writer's objective. Thus the relationship of the story with orature as well as its deviation from orature are to be seen as aesthetic means of influence, as aesthetic expressions of ideology.

However, deviation from the tale structure not only strengthens the message of the story. The interviews I made with the women who had read the story demonstrate that, by projecting Elizabeth's situation as hopeless, and showing how she is doomed to be annihilated

---

8. D. Paulme, "Un conte de fées afriquain: Le garçon travesti ou Joseph en Afrique," *L'Homme* 3: 5–21, and *La mère dévorante* (Paris: Gallimard, 1976) 19–50.

in a patriarchal society with suicide as the only alternative, the story became an instrument for discouraging women and conveying to them the idea that women cannot manage alone. Thus, its deviation from the tale structure also made it a "discourse" of women's oppression.

If the end of "Elizabeth" had been adapted to the traditional tale structure, the story might instead have become a "discourse" of women's liberation. But a "discourse" that challenged the "status quo" would not have fitted into a norm-guarding writer's production.

In traditional society it was important that a woman's labour and reproductive capability remained with her own community. Therefore, girls had to be taught not to listen to strangers, no matter how attractive and friendly these strangers were. Hence, the amount of monster tales aimed at frightening the girls. In modern Kenyan society, increasing teenage pregnancies and children born out of wedlock are a tremendous social problem. The sugar daddy system, which means that elderly wealthy and powerful men exploit the survival needs of young women and, thus, force the girls into temporary sexual relationships and prostitution, is widespread. Therefore, girls have to be taught not to listen to these men, no matter how fatherly and generous they are. Therefore, there are so many modern stories by women writers about rape and unwanted pregnancies. Thus, when related to the concerns of the respective societies where they were produced and reproduced, both the tale and the story prove to be instruments of socialisation, "discourses" of persuasion to guard and protect society.

As norm-guarding writers stress the norm-guarding function of orature, norm-breaking women writers have been inspired by norm-breaking tendencies in orature. These are tendencies that might be expressions of a progressive woman's creative individuality. Norm-breaking women writers question the conventional norm system. They try to extend the limits of the African woman's traditional gender role. They feel solidarity with the underprivileged majority of the women. As stereotyped images of women legitimize and strengthen the oppression of women these women writers call for authentic projections of African women and their conditions. Their aim is twofold:

— changing the negative attitudes of society towards women who try to adapt their traditional gender role to a society in transition, and

— raising women's consciousness, not only of their oppression but also of their potential.

My assumption is that norm-breaking literature is liberating. As a majority of Kenyan women are rural and illiterate women, and as it is also these women that are most oppressed, this category of informants was of particular interest to me in the investigation I have conducted as to indigenous women's literature in Kenyan women's liberation struggle. Because these women could not understand English, the language in which the stories were written, the stories were told to them in the indigenous languages. Let me describe two of these case studies in this field of "listener-response criticism."

The first case study concerns Grace Ogot's story "The Other Woman," as told to a group of Kamba women in Machakos district.[9] The story is about a young married upper middle class couple with two children, living in Nairobi. The wife, who is a secretary, is, despite servants, tired from enduring the double burden of responsibilities to both her family and her job. The crucial problem is that she is too tired to make love to her husband as often as he wants. He gives her no support but, in fact, encourages her to give up her much-wanted job. She is also unfortunate with her *ayahs* (maids). One after the other they get pregnant and have to be fired. The wife suspects the cook to be the culprit, whose own wife and family live in another region. She fires him, too, despite his protests. One day the young wife discovers her husband in bed with an *ayah*. Trying to kill the girl with a knife she misses and cuts off the girl's ear. The maimed and naked girl runs out of the house and disappears for good, but the story and the marriage continue. The young wife realizes it is *her* fault that her husband has been unfaithful. The story ends in the following words: "If you have no time for him, he will go to another woman."

After finishing the story the storyteller asked the audience: "What can we learn from this story?" I had thought that the women would take the sides of the servants, the protagonists that belonged to their own class. But they didn't. They accepted the categories they were familiar with. The class perspective did not count on a grass roots level. It is too abstract. The grass roots women, with their own expe-

---

9. "The Other Woman" is published in Grace Ogot, *The Other Woman* (Nairobi: Transafrica Publishers, 1976).

rience of irresponsible men, identified with the wife. To illustrate what "men are like"one of the women told a story out of her own experience:

> One day her husband had come home together with a male friend and this man's girl friend. He ordered a goat to be slaughtered. While preparing the meal the wife eventually found out that the girl was, in fact, her own husband's girl friend. Wild with fury she tried to kill the girl with her panga. But the girl managed to escape and so did the male guest. The wife then beat her husband up, locked him in the house and put fire to the house. The husband screamed for help and the neighbours came running and rescued him. The married couple then went to the police, where the wife asked the policeman what he would do, if his wife brought a man to their home pretending that this man was her woman friend's lover—while he was, in fact, her own lover. "Kill them both," was the answer. When the policeman then heard what had happened, he identified with the grass roots woman and not with her husband. Since he could see the events from the woman's perspective he declared her not guilty.

A woman being found not guilty is a rare phenomenon in Kenya. Listening to this true life story the other women in the group drilled and cheered their sister who was very pleased with their admiration.

The majority of the educated women who had read "The Other Woman" did not agree that the wife was to be blamed for her husband's raping the *ayahs*. Still, they considered the end of the story happy, as they meant that the wife had been sensible and listened to reason.

Let us now include another class perspective into the analysis. As a member both of the parliament and the government, Grace Ogot is a prominent representative of the prevailing power constellation of her country and, thus, may be regarded as its mouthpiece. In an interview with her, she explained her intentions concerning "The Other Woman." She mentioned her concerns about modern family life in Kenya and the situation of the young generation of educated, professional working wives. Despite her double work load, Grace Ogot said, the wife must never let her husband suspect that she doesn't devote herself to him fully. Neither must she forget that her husband is the pillar of the family.

In the light of the writerly objectives, it is interesting to compare the responses of the rural grass roots women both with the message of the story and the responses of the educated urban women. While the urban middle class wife of the story gives in and puts the blame for her husband's unfaithfulness on herself—and the middle class women readers considered this sensible, though not correct—the grass roots woman introduced above revolted and punished her unfaithful husband. For this she was not only cheered by her sisters but obtained full redress and recognition of her society, which is symbolized by the verdict. According to the message of Grace Ogot's story, women should not break the norms of patriarchal class society. But the grass roots women did not listen to this message. Instead they created another story with a norm-breaking and liberating message.

"How did it come about," I asked my interpreter, "that the wife managed to beat up her husband?" The interpreter answered: "Because women are stronger than men." I don't know whether this is true. But it is a widely spread belief in Kenya. Also one should add that at the same time as a great part of peasant and working class women are socialized into a subordinate gender role and ignorant of their rights, many of them are, in fact, more liberated in mind and more independent of their men than the urban upper and middle class women. This liberating potential seems to be higher among the underprivileged women.[10]

There are several reasons for this, not the least economic and social. A great number of underprivileged women are in practice single mothers. They are used to accepting the entire responsibility for the support of themselves and their children. Even if the husband stays with the family, he is often more of a burden to his wife. Thus, many women, despite children, prefer not to marry since they have nothing to gain from a marriage. These women are strong because they have to be. They can expect little, if any, support from society, and western development strategies often fail to incorporate them.

A privileged minority of women are married to men who have a good position in society. Because of their husbands' high income many of these women, though educated, do not work professionally. They are upper and middle class wives, to use western terminology. If they work professionally, their economic contribution to the family's well being is still much smaller than the contribution of their husbands. Since they benefit socially and economically from a marriage within the élite, most of these women are interested in preserving the status quo in their private sphere, as well as in the political and economic sphere of society. Consequently, they act as norm-guarders.

---

10. See for example C. Obbo, *African Women. Their Struggle for Independence* (London: Zed Press, 1980).

An analysis of the responses and interpretations of the educated women, including that of the writer and the grass roots women, yields class-related, thought-provoking results which, however, seem logical against the background presented here: the stories of the educated women appear conservative, women-oppressive "discourses," while the stories of the illiterate women appeared to be "discourses" of women's liberation.

The second case study from my field work among illiterate rural women, is based on a story by a norm-breaking writer. Her name is Sharfun Rajabali. She is a Kenyan of Asian origin and lives on the coast north of Mombasa. Rajabali is not a professional writer of fiction but an artist and a teacher of art at a teachers' training college. Her story, which is called "The Head of the Family," is not available in Kenya.[11]

"The Head of the Family" is about a woman squatter, called Mukabi, and her struggle for survival against nature, and against society since she wants to be declared the legal owner of the plot she has cultivated. Mukabi's husband, Kathamba, abandoned her and their children when migrating to town several years ago. When he hears that the government is carrying out a land settlement scheme in the district, however, he turns up again to claim the title to land he has never touched with a hoe. Through tremendous efforts Mukabi has the plot registrered in her own name, and thus becomes head of the family not only practically but also legally. And Katahamba returns to the city.

In the midst of the somewhat revolutionary atmosphere that characterized the discussion following the telling of the story one of the eldest women stood up straight and tall, a commanding figure with a strong voice and a twinkle in her eyes. Her first words were: "Mukabi did the right thing when she threw the man out. That's

11. "The Head of the Family" is included in *Whispering Land*, an anthology of short stories published by SIDA in 1985. The anthology was a result of a short story competition for women in Africa arranged by SIDA. For various reasons the official at SIDA who was responsible for the contest and the anthology lost interest in the project and the anthology was never disseminated. The books are stored at SIDA and can be obtained at the price of 40 SEK. For further information on the contest, the work of the jury, and consequences of the contest which may explain why the books were never disseminated, see E. Nicodemus, "Who Owns Third World Women's Knowledge?," *Economic and Political Weekly*, July 12, 1986, 1197–1201. Evelyn Nicodemus was the African member of the jury.

what I did, too." She then told about her own fate which parallelled Mukabi's: her husband had migrated to the city, leaving her with eight children. She wore herself to the bone, scraping a living out of the earth as a squatter, and heard that her husband had built a new family. In 1962, however, when a land settlement scheme was to be carried out in her district, granting squatters title deed to five acres of land each, her husband had returned. But when she succeeded in having her plot registered in the eldest son's name, her husband disappeared back to the city, never to be heard from again.

The old woman finished by saying that if Kathamba had been granted the title deed, he would most likely have sold it and returned to the city with the money, leaving Mukabi and the children penniless. Her audience shouted with joy and cried out: "You are Mukabi! Your name is now Mukabi!" —"Yes," said the old woman proudly, "from now on my name shall be Mukabi and everyone shall call me Mukabi."

Indigenous women's literature had made these rural women understand their own situation and realize that it was not unique, but shared by women all over the country. It gave them a feeling of affinity with Kenyan women of other ethnic groups on a broad national level. Learning how a woman in their own situation managed to master her new situation gave them strategies to cope with their changing environment; it gave them hope and strength.

Since the rural women in my study live in an oral culture, it was not surprising that western theories proved insufficient for analyses of their responses and interpretations. Stanley Fish's and M. Crawford's/R. Chaffin's theories were of particular importance[12] only when supplemented with orature-relevant considerations. Rajabali's story, it seems, reflects the the practices of indigenous orature. This is probably the reason for the rural women's high estimation of the story. They recognized the strong and active heroine of the story who resembled the heroines of orature. Out of oral cultures develop literary characters that are colourful and easy to remember. Colourless literary personalities cannot survive in oral cultures.

Another orature-related reason for the success of "The Head of the Family" was its didactic slant. Even if the women experienced the

---

12. See S. Fish, *Is There a Text in This Class?* (Cambridge, Massachusetts: Harvard University Press, 1980); M. Crawford and R. Chaffin, "The Reader's Construction of Meaning: Cognitive Research on Gender and Comprehension," *Gender and Reading* (Baltimore: John Hopkins University Press, 1986) 3–30.

story session as entertainment, in their culture orature was the most important medium of education. They regard fiction as a knowledge to be acquired. It was for them a means to improve their lives. "The Head of the Family" conveyed knowledge that the women considered valuable. Therefore it was received with acclamation. "The Other Woman" by Ogot, on the other hand, conveyed learning that they would not consume without having revised it—in contrast to the writer's intentions.

Thirdly, "The Head of the Family" is spiced with comments by the writer, such as "Why should women always have the heaviest burden?" This stylistic device appealed to the illiterate women. Used to exchanges between storytellers and their audiences the women accepted the writer's invitation to a dialogue. They were able to enter the co-actors' part in the story session. They had, as usual in traditional orature, become co-creators in a drama performance. There is every reason to believe that this active participation on behalf of the audience strengthened the liberating effect of the "discourse." To these grass roots women Rajabali's story was, no doubt, a "discourse" of women's liberation.

This chapter, based on a limited number of case studies, should not be used as a foundation for general conclusions. However, by analyzing political dimensions embedded in various "discourse" levels of indigenous orature and modern women's literature in Kenya, it may have shed some light on the potential role of indigenous women's literature in the Kenyan women's liberation struggle, thereby also pointing to the impact of orature's relevance in modern literature for rural illiterate women. Taking as its starting-point the norm-guarding and the norm-breaking lines in orature, the chapter has indicated continuity between Kenyan orature and modern women's writing, concerning the structure, the content and the function in society. Finally, it has demonstrated how a text, when presented to readers and listeners in different socio-cultural environments or "interpretative communities," is reproduced with different, even contradictory, meanings.

In Search of Achebe's Dignity; or, The Cauliflower Episode

Adewale Maja-Pearce

It was at a confererence held in the Scandinavian Institute of African Studies, a quarter of a century ago, that Wole Soyinka castigated his fellow writers for what he called their lack of vision. "In the movement towards chaos in modern Africa," he said:

> ... the writer did not anticipate .... He was content to turn his eye backwards in time and prospect in archaic fields for forgotten gems which would dazzle and distract. But never inwards, never truly into the present, never into the obvious symptoms of the niggling, warning predictable present from which alone lay the salvation of ideals.[1]

Soyinka had in mind the then-dominant school of Nigerian writing, which had set itself the task of rescuing the African past from the distortions of the imperialist chroniclers. The most celebrated of all these writers was, of course, Chinua Achebe, whose first novel, *Things Fall Apart*, was published in 1958. Over the next ten years, it seemed, every other novel was busy unearthing forgotten gems to dazzle and distract from the slaughter that was about to take place in the name of Biafra.

Twenty-five years later, there is no shortage of novels dealing with the niggling, warning, predictable present, but to what end? Nigeria, today, is in a worse state than at the time of Independence in 1960, and this despite the incredible good fortune of oil. And what is true of Nigeria is equally true of the continent as a whole. Wars and rumours of wars indeed, but you can add famine, dictatorship and religious strife that are currently putting millions of lives at risk.

What went wrong? If it was possible for Soyinka to lay the blame squarely (or even partly) on the shoulders of the Achebe school of Nigerian literature, on the grounds that they refused to look at what

---

1. Wole Soyinka, "The Writer in a Modern African State," in Per Wästberg ed. *The Writer in Modern Africa* (Uppsala: Nordiska afrikainstitutet, 1968) 17.

was happening under their noses, what do we say when the stench from the continent positively seeps off the pages of one novel after another, to no visible effect?

Part of the answer is to be found in Achebe's own justification for his archeological excavations. In an essay he wrote after the event, he spoke in terms of salvaging the dignity of the hitherto despised African, as follows:

> This theme—put quite simply—is that African people did not hear of culture for the first time from Europeans; that their societies were not mindless but frequently had a philosophy of great depth and beauty and, above all, they had dignity.[2]

What this—simply—amounted to was a rather misty-eyed account of pre-colonial African societies in which the gods, the ancestors and the elders swapped proverbs over calabashes of palm-wine until the arrival of the white man, with his Bible and his literacy and his scorn for the bits and pieces of wood which weren't really gods at all (let alone ancestors), simply—bits and pieces of wood.

Dignity, in short, turned out to be a Golden Age of perfect order and harmony; but the point isn't that people should be denied their myths, only that they shouldn't mistake these myths for the real thing. The African past may or may not have been as idyllic as Achebe & Co. would have us believe, but the white man *did* arrive, the past *was* disrupted, and one of the consequences of all this was that Achebe et al were now busy writing their novels—in English. Moreover, their novels were attempting to prove what was not susceptible of proof in the first place, since the matter of the African's dignity—or, more accurately, their humanity—was never up for grabs. The onus was on the Other to prove that Africans were somehow inferior, morally speaking; the onus was never on the African to prove that this was not so. And in attempting to disprove a negative, which is what the entire exercise amounted to, the writers were evading the central question: that of the relationship between Africa and Europe at a level which goes beyond simple rage at the racial hurt.

Let me put it as simply—Achebe's word—as possible: Europe was able to colonise Africa because Europe was the modern world.

---

2. Chinua Achebe, "The Role of a Writer in a New Nation," in G. D. Killam ed. *African Writers on African Writing* (London: Heinemann Educational Books, 1973) 8.

Everybody suspects this but nobody says so; and the strategy that the Nigerian writer has adopted in order to avoid looking the unpleasant fact in the face is to pretend that the modern world is an inconvenient fiction of the European imagination.

The easiest way of achieving this particular state of nirvana is to ignore the modern world altogether and go prospecting in archaic fields, but always with the instruments of the modern world. The English novel, after all, is the expression of a modern, bourgeois sensibility. It is rational, progressive and secular. It was never fashioned as an instrument with which to go rooting around in archaic fields, nor was it concerned with the elaborate pantheon of archaic gods (and never mind the ancestors) who were pressed into service by the Achebe school as proof positive that Africans were human beings.

The more complicated way of achieving the same end is to pretend that the modern world has nothing to tell you, even on the few occasions when Europe is admitted. But always by the back door, as it were, and only then as a variation of Achebe's dignity. Let me give an example.

In Kole Omotoso's *The Edifice*, Dele is a Nigerian student in London about to return home. To this end, he has just received a letter from his mother warning him not to cross her threshold with a white wife, a notion which appears to affront him even as he reads the letter. "Imagine mother thinking I could ever descend to marry a white girl!" he exclaims. "What a thought!" "How would a white woman be beautiful?"[3] Well, each to their own; and yet, curiously enough, he proceeds to do exactly this, for reasons which become all too clear in the course of the ensuing narrative.

No sooner does he arrive in Nigeria with Daisy, his bride, than he starts behaving in the most atrocious possible manner:

> He pushed me down. I banged against the french window. He hit out wildly and his punch caught me on the left side of my head. I reeled and fell down. He began to kick me, mechanically, not caring where. I remember his feet making contact from one moment to another.[4]

It isn't enough that Dele should behave like this—wife-beating, after all, is not an exclusively African preserve, or even tradition—but that

---

3. Kole Omotoso, *The Edifice* (London: Heinemann Educational Books, 1971) 49.
4. *Ibid*. 103.

Daisy must herself participate in her debasement, which is why the author makes her recount it herself. "Please, Dele," the poor woman implores him at one point, "how did your grandfather's wives plead with him? Did they call him their lord, the commander of all their wishes?"[5] But he hasn't finished with her yet: "One night I heard voices in his bedroom. There was a thin black girl in bed with him. It was a shock to me. How could he do it? Did he not love me? Was I not carrying his child?"[6]

At this point, one would have thought, even the most docile of women would have called it a day. Not so this modern, middle-class, university-educated, 1960s Englishwoman: "I accepted that part of Dele having girlfriends," she says, *"and even of his bringing them into the same bed in which our unborn baby had been conceived"*[7] (my italics). And then—the final, improbable twist—she gives birth to a son, who is promptly whisked away to the village, there to be murdered, presumably because this half-caste-mixed-breed-neither-black-nor-white and, probably, self-hating mulatto might conceivably grow up to express a preference for cauliflower cheese, of which more in a moment.

In the meantime, it might have been better for all concerned if the author had deliberately set out to write a piece of pornography; if, indeed, Dele was simply the familiar black stud who never fails to ravish the delicate English flower at the first available opportunity, thereby spoiling her forever. "I'm half-crazy, all for the love of you," this particular flower declares elsewhere.[8] But, of course, she has now partaken of the forbidden fruit, and can no more do without it than she can object to the murder of her son. In either case, she is no longer a woman, just the object of a demeaning fantasy which will somehow compensate for the loss of dignity consequent on the European adventure, and for which she is made to pay—literally— with her own flesh: Go ye forth into the white man's house and grab his woman, would have been a more accurate injunction to those about to depart Africa's shores in search of the Golden Locks.

But nothing, mind you, about what you actually see when you get there, only concern to simplify and therefore betray what is admit-

---

5. *Ibid.* 100.
6. *Ibid.* 112.
7. *Ibid.* 112.
8. *Ibid.* 102.

tedly a complex inheritance. In this regard, African writers have been left far behind by their Caribbean colleagues, by Derek Walcott and V.S. Naipaul and C.L.R. James, all of whom have understood the true nature of their heritage. I am aware, of course, that Walcott has been heartily abused by certain sections of the Caribbean intelligentsia, just as I'm aware that Naipaul's name is mud among an even larger section of the African intelligentsia; but bearing in mind James's own dictum, that "one is an accident, two is a coincidence and three is a movement," I'm bound to recognise an extraordinary achievement when I see one.

The reason for this achievement is already suggested by the fact that the Caribbean writer has no choice in this matter of language, and must make the language—and therefore the history of the language—his own. And I mean language in the deeper sense; in the sense in which, to quote F.R. Leavis, "Language ... does more than provide an analogue for a culture ... it is largely the essential life of a culture." The consequences of the African failure to do the same was most dramatically illustrated by the events in Liberia last year, and by the current estimates of the number of Africans who will die from hunger this year. Meanwhile, anyone who tries to dig a little bit deeper, to accept the facts of history as they are and not as one would wish them, can expect the following.

I have published an extended essay, *How many miles to Babylon?*, in which I attempt to examine my relationship with Britain, my mother's country and my home for the last twenty years. In the course of the book, I tried to examine what we mean by the terms "race," "culture" and "ethnicity"; who is British and who isn't, and on whose say-so? I knew I was British, but of an odd variety, just as I knew I was Nigerian, but of an equally odd variety: three years previously, I had published a travel-essay on Nigeria, my father's country, in which I had attempted to ask the same sorts of questions.

No sooner did the book appear than the heaven's fell. In the pages of a London-based Nigerian weekly newspaper (since defunct, I'm happy to report) I came across an extended review under the ominous title: "Adewale Maja-Pearce is sick ... mother, help your son." Clearly, the reviewer, Gordon Tialobi, was going to pull out all the stops. I wasn't disappointed. Claiming to have unearthed incontrovertible evidence that Adewale Maja-Pearce was suffering from an advanced case of that well-known disease, self-hatred, Mr. Tialobi duly declared:

The book, in essence, invites us to share Mr Maja-Pearce's journey to discover that he is English after all, even though he may have had a black Nigerian father, and therefore only half white (*sic*). Cogent reasons for identifying himself with his white English half are advanced as forcefully as the pathological (Oedipal?) hate he expresses for his father and his father's country....[9]

To clinch his argument, Mr Tialobi reproduces the following passage from the book:

> I had eaten cauliflower cheese in Nigeria but it was prepared by Alexander, our cook, at my mother's insistence, and he didn't have any idea what it should look or even taste like. To Alexander it was hardly proper ... food. My mother, who hated waste or perhaps wanted to maintain the fiction that she could have an everyday meal in the tropics, pretended that everything was fine. Everything wasn't fine. It tasted awful.[10]

In the context of the book, this passage was supposed to work on a number of different levels; but it is enough, for our purposes, that I wanted to bring out a certain poignancy which I see repeated in reverse in Britain, where Nigerians (above all, Nigerians!), attempting to negotiate the pain of exile, will prepare a makeshift meal in order to make-believe that they really are at home; that they aren't sitting around a kitchen table thousands of miles from home and missing it like hell. All very human and all very harmless; but Mr Tialobi, who is perhaps above such ordinary expressions of simple humanity, chooses instead to extrapolate only sinister undertones, as follows:

> The sad thing about the cauliflower episode is that, without realising it, Mr Pearce was explaining why many English women's marriages (and probably his mother?) to Nigerians often fail. Cosy in their superior Englishness, they neither accept, integrate, compromise, nor adjust to the environmental needs of their husbands' land. Many often carry their arrogance to extremes, refusing their husbands to eat Nigerian dishes because of the foreign smell. Their children mock their fathers' languages, eventually growing up to speak disparagingly (like Adewale Maja-Pearce does) of their fathers' countries.[11]

Vulgar, nasty little man; but the pity of it is that Mr. Tialobi could have chosen a more revealing passage than the one he did if he was so concerned to prove that Adewale Maja-Pearce gloried in certain

---

9. *Nigeria HomeNews*, June 28–July 4, 1990, 10.
10. Adewale Maja-Pearce, *How many miles to Babylon?* (London: Heinemann, 1990) 30.
11. *Nigeria HomeNews* 10.

aspects of his Britishness. Language, for instance, and with it the tradition out of which the language springs. But then I can no more deny Europe than I can deny Africa, since I so obviously partake of both. In fact, however, my position is no more attenuated than Mr. Tialobi's. All Africans partake of Europe for very straightforward historical reasons; and African writers who write in English can only pretend otherwise by banging the African drum as loudly as possible, the better to drown out what they know to be the truth.

Mr Tialobi's sentiments in his review are extreme but not unusual; and the unwillingness or the inability of the African writer to explore the complexity of the African heritage has only reinforced the marginalisation about which they so vociferously complain. Nobody listens to Africa, they say, but then, thirty years after Independence, Africa says very little that anybody needs to hear. Not even, alas, the cry for help as men dressed up in women's bathrobes fired their guns into a continent, reminiscent of the colonialists themselves when Joseph Conrad took a trip into the heart of darkness nearly one hundred years ago:

> Pop, would go one of the six-inch guns; a small flame would dart and vanish, a tiny projectile would give a feeble screech—and nothing happened. Nothing could happen. There was a touch of insanity in the proceeding, a sense of lugubrious drollery in the sight; and it was not dissipated by somebody on board assuring me earnestly that there was a camp of natives—he called them enemies!—hidden out of sight somewhere.[12]

---

12. Joseph Conrad, *Heart of Darkness* (Oxford: University Press, 1990) 152.

The Islamic Architecture and Art in Sub-Saharan Africa: A Problem of Identity

Karin Ådahl

The *umma* of Islam does not only mean confessing to the same religion but also sharing the patterns of daily life. The religious rules and duties affect the individual as well as the traditions of society, and Islam, as a consequence, also signifies a civilization and a culture.

In the architecture and arts of Islamic society, common expressions have developed in different regions that relate to religious life and the importance of the Koran and the Arabic script with its strong ornamental character. The Koran is studied by all Muslims in Arabic, even in non-Arabic speaking countries, and every Muslim develops at least a certain understanding of and feeling for the Arabic script and its particular importance in relation to religion. The impact of the Koran in the Muslim world as a guide to every moment in life and the Koran as Allah's own word cannot therefore be overestimated.

Mosque architecture is of course closely related to the cult and the religious service. In most Muslim countries it also developed according to the plan of the first mosque in the Islamic world, at Medina.

Islamic art has expressed itself most characteristically through the use of the Arabic script in its many calligraphic forms and through the abstract ornament in geometric forms. Also of importance is a reluctance to represent human beings in a three-dimensional, or even two dimensional form, although this suggestion has often been exaggerated, and misinterpreted as a prohibition by non-Muslims.

Sources

The studies of Islamic architecture and art in sub-Saharan Africa present many problems. Since it has only recently been developed as a field of research there is still an embarrassing lack of published material.

The only comprehensive survey of Islamic monuments in the African continent is the illustrated catalogue in G. Mitchell's *Islamic Architecture*.[1] The most important recent studies have been carried out by Labelle Prussin in her book *Hatumere; Islamic Design in West Africa*, where she examines the concept of how Islamic culture expresses itself in the design, architecture, and art of West Africa.[2] A more systematic analysis of West African architecture has been undertaken by S. Domian in *Architecture Soudanaise*.[3] While an outline of the history of Islamic architecture in sub-Saharan Africa may be drawn from the existing monuments, it is more difficult to establish a basis for a chronology and a typology of Islamic art. In *Hatumere* Prussin attempts to cover all aspects of artistic expression, especially the ornament. Rene A. Bravmann draws attention in his *African Islam* to certain phenomena as evidence of an Islamic influence on the arts, while his *Islam and Tribal Art in West Africa*, although focused on the African mask, offers a more analytic approach.[4] Since material is insufficient and documents non-existent, it seems hazardous to outline a history of Islamic art. Jan Vansina, however, tries different methods in *Art History in Africa*, which is a study that may offer new openings in understanding the character of Islamic art in black Africa.[5] A common difficulty for the authors appears to be their lack of understanding of what can really be said to be items of art. A strictly art historical analysis has yet to be undertaken.

Islamic architecture

Until recently the mud architecture of West Africa in the so-called Sudanese style ("Sudanese" in this context applies to the savannah belt of sub-Saharan Africa from Senegal to Lake Chad) was considered to be not much more than shelter. Prussin writes:

1. A. Leary, "West Africa" and R. Lewcock, "East Africa" in G. Mitchell (ed.), *Islamic Architecture* (London: Thames and Hudson, 1986) 274–79 and 278–79.
2. Labelle Prussin, *Hatumere: Islamic Design in West Africa* (Berkeley: University of California Press, 1985).
3. S. Domian, *Arcitecture Soudanaise* (Paris: Éditions L'Harmattan, 1989); see also T. Engeström, "Contributions aux connaissances de styles de construction au Soudan Français," *Etnos* 20 (1955): 122–26.
4. Rene A. Bravmann, *African Islam* (Washington: Smithsonian Institution, 1983); *Islam and Tribal Art in West Africa* (Cambridge: Cambridge University Press, 1974).
5. Jan Vansina, *Art History in Africa* (London: Longman, 1984).

... most important is the attitude, shared by architect and layman alike, that building in sub-Saharan Africa is not architecture at all, but at most, building technology, shelter seen only in terms of the techniques which its builders command, and not in terms of the aesthetic value.[6]

The West African mosques, as we see them today, represent a strong and forceful architectural tradition and it is also possible to distinguish different styles and a historical development.

When Islam was introduced and the mosque constructed in the centre of the sub-Saharan African town or village, the presence of the mosque and religious life profoundly influenced the structure of the town and society. While pagan worship was practised in hidden places outside the village with secret rites and magic, when Islam was adopted the place of worship moved into the centre of the village, and prayer was undertaken openly at regular hours in the company of other members of the Muslim community. The place of worship was the religious centre that also became the cultural centre through the institutions connected with the mosque, such as a school, a library, and sometimes a hospital.

The mosque was easily identified by its size, the mass of the walls surrounding the courtyard, the tower on the quibla wall and, most importantly, the minaret. Although of significant size, the mosque is enclosed around its interior functions with little dominance of the entrance gate and with little outward decoration or manifestation. As with the mosque, so with the private house, which similarly encloses the life of the family. All activities are centred around an open courtyard and the building complex is surrounded by walls with few openings. In this context it should be kept in mind that Sharia encourages private property and enhances its protection as distinct from more collectivist systems in pre-Islamic sub-Saharan Africa. This aspect is prominent in towns like Djenné and Timbouctou, but less so in a traditional African village.

The oldest mosques still standing are the Sankoré mosque and Djinguereber mosque in Timbouctou and the tomb-mosque of Askia Muhammed in Gao, all built in the same style and all in Mali. The building material is unfired, oval bricks, or "banco," formed by hand and covered by a smooth coat of mud-cement, sometimes given a pattern by strokes of the hand.

---

6. Prussin, "The Architecture of Islam in West Africa," *African Arts* 1.2 (1968): 32.

The Sudanese style and building technology are related both to architecture in southern Algeria and Mauretiania and to Hausa architecture in Niger, but are still significantly different to these traditions in construction and decorative expression. Most characteristically the mud walls are reinforced with beams of wood or palm tree, protruding from the walls. Originally the beams might have served as a permanent scaffolding but are now part of the aesthetic expression of the building. The mud plaster is renewed every year before the rain season. The walls rise out of the ground, being shaped by the same earthy material, and the courtyard as well as the floor of the prayer room are covered solely by a mixture of earth and sand. Carpets are rolled out during prayer sessions and there are virtually no objects in the mosque. The mihrab is a simple, unardoned niche and the mimbar a small, movable stool. There are no candlesticks or Koran stands, only some simple lamps hanging from the ceiling and in some places electric fans used in the hot season.

The plan of the Sankoré and Djinguereber mosques show the same open courtyard, with the main entrance from the street in the southeast section of the complex. The direction towards Mecca, the quibla, is also indicated in the courtyard by a mihrab in the east wall. From the courtyard a small staircase leads up to the minaret with its wide base and tapering, pyramidal walls and far-protruding beams at regular intervals. The prayer room is rectangular, with aisles parallel to the quibla wall, supported by pillars. There is no articulation or decoration of the arches or the beams.[7] The simplicity and serenity of the construction and the moulded, almost melted shapes, still permit monumentality; the total impression is overwhelmingly forceful. It can be assumed that the original structures of the 14th century mosques have been preserved more or less intact and unchanged through the centuries. It should be noticed that the maintenance of the mosque is a common concern for everybody in the villages or town. The work is undertaken annually according to ritual procedures. The maintenance occasions no reason for change while buildings of more durable material, when being deteriorated, may need reconstruction and are thus more likely to be profoundly rebuilt and changed.

One can assume that the same technology and the same building material of mud, banco, and bricks have been used ever since the

7. Domian 87–93.

The Sankoré mosque
Photo: Karin Ådahl

The Djinguerebe mosque
Photo: Karin Ådahl

early 14th century up to the present day. We can see these features in the modern but traditionally built mosques in Djenné, Mopti and Niono. The size of these buildings is impressive. Their style emphasizes the verticality of the façades by the powerfully rounded pilasters that terminate in turrets and stepped, conical towers. A symbolic meaning has been added to the turrets by their carrying ostrich eggs as spires. The gothic impression which is the result of the monumental size and the repeated verticality of the pilasters of the Djenné mosque reappear in the interior where the long, narrow aisles are united by ogival arches.[8]

The arcades, the double windows, and the minaret of the Niono mosque on the other hand remind one of medieval, Romanesque architecture, which is unexpected in the African setting. It could probably be explained by the fact that the architect had a French background. The Djenné mosque was built in the early 20th century while the Niono mosque is a recent construction—from the 1950s.

The vernacular architecture, constructed in the same mud material in Timbouctou and Djenné, has been influenced by the North African, Arab townscape.

Timbouctou is spread out at the border of the desert with broad streets leading through the town, separating blocks of private houses lined up along narrow streets.[9] The houses are usually built in two storeys, with only the façade visible from the street. The entrance gives access to a courtyard around which the living-rooms are arranged for different purposes. The façade only has windows on the second floor. Peculiar features of Timbouctou are the beehive-shaped ovens in the main streets, for the common use of the people living in the block.

The traditional architecture of Djenné and Timbouctou has been preserved because of the rather difficult access to both towns by road. Djenné is dominated by the mosque, built on a terrace on a vast, open plaza. The streets are narrow and winding with small openings or squares in front of the more important houses. The simple family houses, often in two storeys, are built around a courtyard with no particular importance attached to the façade or the entrance door. There is, however, less seclusion than in the Arab town, since

---

8. J.-L. Bourgeois, "The History of the Great Mosque of Djenné," *African Arts* 20.3 (1987): 54–63.
9. *Toumbouctou*, ed. Comité de Jumelage-Saintes-Toumbouctou, 1986, 41–51.

Mali

Djenné
The mosque, the front
Photo: Karin Ådahl

Djenné
The mosque, the yard
Photo: Karin Ådahl

Niono
The mosque
Photo: Karin Ådahl

there are less strict rules governing the position of women in African Islamic society.

The houses of the learned men are given a special importance by a monumental façade with a *potige*, a framework of pilasters and windows around and above the entrance. The windows of the reception room on the second floor often have horseshoe-arched frames and window grills with geometric star patterns that reveal a Moroccan influence.

Travelling from Mopti to Bamako it can be observed that in the villages, mosques are being built in at least four different styles: the old simple mud architecture with a rectangular nave and a round, conical minaret; the new, Djenné-style, with three towers above the quibla wall and the vertical pilasters articulating the high, although less monumental, walls; the imported Maghreb style, mainly influenced by the Algerian mosque architecture, with a high, slim, square minaret, decorated with geometrical relief patterns in the tradition of the Quttubiya mosque in Marrakesh; and, finally, small mosques in a style which recalls the most basic shape of a Christian missionary church, with a simple, saddle-roofed nave and a slim, slightly tapering minaret attached to the end of the nave.[10]

An example of the Djenné type mosque is that in Téné. Of greater interest is the old mosque of Segou-ko´re (Seko´re), built on a terrace or mound in the centre of a small town. The plan is square, with a rectangular courtyard and a narrow prayer room with only one aisle. The minaret is a small, elevated square platform and the mihrab traditionally indicated by a conical, small tower.

Friday mosques in the major cities in West Africa are now being constructed in a mixture of imported styles, from the Spanish-Morish tradition to the Ottoman style. Some even show influences from Mecca, Medina, Pakistan or India. Moreover, modern and contemporary vernacular architecture in Mali is influenced by traditional mud architecture, especially by that of the Djenné style. Its highly original features with an interplay between the rectangular shape of the building with its flat roof and the vertical effect of the pilasters of the façade and the *potige*, also appear to have influenced the French style in the construction of administration buildings in Bamako. While the style of the vernacular architecture of Timbouctou and Djenné was brought to Bamako and Segou and perfected there, the French devel-

---

10. These observations were made during a visit to Mali in 1990; see also Domian 90–111.

Segou-koré
Village mosque
Photo: Karin Ådahl

Tené
Village mosque
Photo: Karin Ådahl

oped a new "national" style with abundant use of concrete and with modern building technology.

The spectacular shapes and expression of the mud architecture of the traditional mosque was reproduced in full scale to represent Senegal and the A. O. F. at the World Fair in 1922 in Marseille and at the World Exhibition in 1931 in Paris.[11] Also a curiosity is the mosque in Frejus in southern France, built as a small replica of the Djenné mosque.[12]

---

11. Prussin 18–20.
12. N. Beautheac and F.-X. Bouchart, *L'Europe exotique* (Paris: Chêne, 1985) 190–92.

Following from this brief survey of the structural expressions and traditions of West African Islamic architecture, mainly from Mali, I would like to return to the question of the Islamic character and the identity of Islamic architecture. For a more comprehensive study, the architecture of Ghana, Nigeria, Burkina Faso, Guinea, and Niger should also be taken into account. I conclude that Sudanese mud architecture probably extended over a vast area from Senegal to Sudan and that monuments in the Sudanese mud tradition developed different styles through a period of six hundred years. These monuments constitute an important chapter in the history of Islamic architecture. Their style is unique and they were important for the community by and for whom they were built; their Islamic legitimacy cannot be questioned.

More extensive and profound studies and documentation, especially of the lesser-known mosques in small towns and villages, will be important if we are to further the knowledge of the development of the style. Prussin writes:

> When discussing almost any topic relating to the Western Sudan, one fact must be kept in mind: the presence of Islam is a force which pervades all aspects of the community in which it is found. It is Islam as a force that gave rise to the mosques, palaces and tombs found there.[13]

The Islamic *umma* must be taken into account since, as Prussin has also pointed out:

> Ethnographical field work on Africa has been carried out on micro-level, anthropologically oriented and geographically localised ... Ethnograpic provincialism, the result of in-depth study, has deprived him [the anthropologist] of a spatial perspective.[14]

However, one can hardly object that a fuller knowledge about Islamic culture in Africa, in time and space, postulates a conception of the continent as a unity shaped by the interaction of the Islamic and the non-Islamic parts; North Africa in relation to sub-Saharan Africa, and East Africa in relation to West Africa and the Middle East—with Islam being a uniting force.

---

13. Prussin 70.
14. Prussin 132.

Islamic art

As a field of research the Islamic art of sub-Saharan Africa, whether in West Africa or on the East African coast, presents many problems. The first problem is, what is *art* in this context and what is *Islamic* art? The second problem is the scarcity of material. Few objects are preserved which are more than a hundred years old. Furthermore, objects are not dated or related to events or persons. The third problem is that it is a field of research which has only recently attracted scholars. Therefore, as mentioned above, literature is scarce and the methods of analysing art possibly having an Islamic character have not yet been developed.

By which criteria could we distinguish Islamic art from the "tribal" art of Africa? Or should we accept all items of art produced in Muslim society and by Muslims as Islamic art?

Art reflects man's thoughts, ideas, needs, and relations to his surroundings. Through a form, an image, an ornament, or a decoration the artist creates a language by which he expresses, in visual form, what he wants to communicate to the world around him. He creates from his experience and imagination and he is himself guided by the world he inhabits. A shape, an image, or an ornament is born out of previously existing shapes, images, and ornaments. The artist himself and his art are products of the cultural setting in which they exist. Subsequently, art in an Islamic environment is then inevitably affected by Islamic thought and artistic tradition.

Islamic art is generally characterized by the use of decorative ornament, geometric or vegetal, in abstract forms; by the frequent use of calligraphic inscriptions; by the absence of three-dimensional sculpture. There is no art for art's sake; artistic expression and creativity are related to functional objects and objectives. Islamic art is manifest in illuminated manuscripts, in minute paintings, in decorated and glazed ceramic wares, and in decorated metalwork, wooden objects, glass, textiles, and carpets. The language of so-called "classical" Islamic art has become familiar through the arabesque and the use of the calligraphy, the floral and vegetal patterns, and the two-dimensional images of human beings and animals. The most characteristic feature is arguably the relative absence of three-dimensional sculpture. The ceramic production is simple and appears to have been so through the centuries. A reason for this—as well as the use of un-fired bricks for construction—is the lack of wood for the kilns where only low temperatures can be obtained which excludes any fabrication of finer or glazed ceramic wares.

The objects which most clearly express the aesthetics of Muslim societies in Africa are the woven textiles with geometric patterns, the embroideries often with symbolic meaning, the ornamented woodwork, and, as an exception, geometrically decorated Nupe metalwork in Nigeria.[15] On discussing the matter with a museum director in Mali and putting the question to him of what he considered to be Islamic art in Mali society his answer was "the tomb stones." The Muslim tomb stones are inscribed with calligraphic Koranic text with an obvious aesthetic value but may not generally be classified as art objects.

There is still no systematic analysis of the ornament in Islamic art in sub-Saharan Africa, although Prussin pays more attention to the ornament and, in particular, to the so-called Hausa knot, which is frequently used in ornamental decoration in West Africa. The Hausa knot also appears, as Bravmann has pointed out, in the illumination of Koran manuscripts along with geometric ornaments, usually in shades of brown and red of a distinctly African character.[16] Bravmann also discusses the use of calligraphy on Quranic wooden boards, the geometric ornament of the Tuareg amulets and textiles, carved wooden objects and the representation of Buraq, the mythical horse with a woman's head who carried Muhammed· through the seven skies.[17] Like Vansina in *Art History in Africa*, Bravmann also analyses the use of the mask in the Islamic society of West Africa. The mask was accepted by the Muslim rulers and clergy in as early as the 14th century, as we know from the Ibn Battuta who, in his *Travels* describes the masked poets at the court of the king at Niani in Mali.[18] The wooden masks are often inscribed on the inside with an Arabic text from the Koran or with a magical formula, which is intended to please Allah as well as the animist powers. The mask cannot however, to my opinion, be considered an Islamic art object, in spite of the Arabic script.

---

15. Bravmann, *African Islam* 88–92.
16. *Ibid*. 21.
17. *Ibid*. 73 ff.; see also N. R. Mickelsen, "Tuareg Jewelry," *African Arts* 9.2 (1976): 16–19.
18. *Islams vandringsmän, Ibn Battuta, "Arabvärldens Marco Polo" 1325–1354* (translated into Swedish from the ed. of Sir H. A. R. Gibb) (Stockholm: Hallonbergen, 1989).

The attempts of Bravmann, Vansina and Prussin to define the expressions of Islamic art in sub-Saharan Africa have brought to light material and created an awareness of the problem of the Islamic identity in the arts and architecture in black Africa which is an important point of departure for further research in a field which is still in its infancy.

The Actor, the Art of Acting and Liminality

Kacke Götrick

The existence of tragedy and comedy in traditional African theatre has long been debated. As I have shown elsewhere the relevance of the Aristotelian concepts of tragedy and comedy is limited as far as traditional African theatre is concerned (Götrick 1992). Some of the problems that feature in this debate originate in the Western notion that one performance belongs to one genre only. Such an expectation has made many blind to the fact that several traditional African theatres are characterized by their use of a varying number of dramas of different genres in a performance. Thus, a performance may contain two or more genres. The genres of the different theatre traditions are, of course, not identical, but they seem to share some basic properties (*ibid.*).

Generally speaking, many traditional African theatres seem to employ two broad groups of genre, and maybe a variety of mixtures between these two.[1] And the difference between these two groups is basically constituted by their relation to a superhuman realism (Götrick 1992).

One genre, often labelled tragedy, ritual or sacred drama, is of particular interest to the art of acting, because some of its properties demand from the actors a very specific capacity not found in Western actors. The genre is characterized by a property which to Westerners falls outside the category of theatre, namely a relation to a superhuman realm that is expected to give a result lasting beyond the performance. This means that the action is expected to be religiously efficacious. In order to achieve this end, the actor performs on the stage as a priest would do in his surroundings. The actor does not imitate, and the acting is not mimetic.

If this non-mimetic genre is seen as one pole, then the contrasting pole is a genre characterized by mimesis. As far as mimesis is concerned, this contrasting genre does not demand from the actors any-

---

1. This cautious expression depends on the fact that our knowledge of the genres and their properties is still very limited.

thing different from what is demanded by Western theatre. It is interesting to note—and important to keep in mind—that traditional African theatres at times employ non-mimetic as well as mimetic genres in the same performance.

Against this background the issue of the art of acting immediately comes to mind. And many questions arise. Does this kind of acting involving non-mimetic, religious performance require a type of actor with a capability or capacity that is different from that of his Western colleague? If the answer is in the affirmative, what implications does it have for the meeting between traditional and modern theatre? Is it possible for modern theatre, performed by modern actors, to achieve the same effect as achieved by traditional actors? Are the modern written drama and the dramatist affected in any way?

A crucial factor here is the actor's relation to a superhuman realm. The actor is meant to function as a mediator between the two realms, the human and the superhuman. In order to fulfil this function the actor must be able to cross the border between the realms. So it follows that he is liminal.

This liminality, however, is not objectively perceivable but can be observed only through the beliefs of the actors and the spectators. Hence audience perception is as crucial to a study of this kind as an investigation of the actors. After all, the art of the actor rests on conventions shared with the audience, and the notions of liminality and religious efficacy are parts of these conventions.

To discuss some of the questions asked above in a more relevant way, there is a need for descriptions of the art of acting from the point of view of some of the basic theatre conventions on which it is founded. To this end I will give a survey of some of the theatre traditions of the Yoruba people, namely the Egungun Apidan, the Gelede and the Obatala ritual drama. Rather than making generalizations about many theatre traditions from different cultures, possibly with their individual arts of acting, I prefer to restrict myself to one ethnic group, since this will allow for some details. With this survey as a background I will discuss some of the problems involved in stage productions of a modern drama about a superhuman realm.

THE ACTOR IN THE TRADITIONAL THEATRE

Acting in Africa is an old activity, indeed an old profession. Professional actors appeared in the Apidan theatre of the Yoruba people probably as early as the end of the 17th century.[2]

The Egungun Apidan theatre: origin

The Apidan theatre[3] emerged from the religious Egungun Society, which probably came into existence in the second half of the 16th century (see Babayemi 1980, 23f., Law 1977, 43). The emergence of the Apidan theatre is likely to have occurred in the following century.[4] Some evidence shows that the Apidan theatre was well established as an artistic entity by the end of the 18th century.[5] It emerged and developed at the Court of the Alaafin, the king, but later, during

---

2. It should be emphasized that the Apidan theatre with its art of acting is not the only relevant tradition in Nigeria, let alone in Africa. The Koteba of the Bamana people in Mali is another example.

3. The theatre is also called Onidan and Alaarinjo. *Apidán* means a person who performs tricks (*idán* = an artful trick, magic, wonder). *Onídán* means a person who has tricks, and *Aláàrìnjó* means a person who dances as he walks. The troupe leaders I have talked to want to be called Apidan or Onidan but not Alaarinjo, which is understandable, because the latter label "originated as an abuse," as Adedeji says (1969, 191 and 1978, 34). Adedeji also says that the troupes were called Alaarinjo only in the Ibadan empire (1969, 178 note 104). But not even the Ibadan-based troupes of today want to be known by that name. Hence I prefer Apidan.

4. Joel Adedeji uses oral history for information on the founding of the Apidan theatre. He attributes the founding to one Ologbin Ologbojo, who, on uncovering a conspiracy, made some masquerades act as entertainers (Adedeji, 1978, 27–29; 1970, 81–82; 1969, 133–38. See also Johnson, 1973, 164–66). This event took place shortly before 1600 (Law, 1977, 43 and 59), and led, according to Adedeji, to the establishment of one Olugbere Agan as the "leader of a band of 'costumed-players' set up at Court" and to his becoming "the first professional actor" (Adedeji, 1969, 101f. See also Adedeji 1978, 30). But Adedeji also names as the first professional actor one Esa Ogbin, who lived probably at the end of the 18th century.

5. Indirectly Babayemi (1980, 26) states that the entertainers were organized well before a particular contest arranged by Alaafin Abiodun took place. Abiodun reigned effectively 1774–1789, according to Law (1977, 60). And further, the standard and organisation of the performance witnessed by Clapperton 1826 in Old Oyo, or Katunga as he calls it, presupposes a long process of maturing (see Clapperton, 1829, 53–56).

the unrest and internal wars of the 19th century, it spread far beyond the courts and into the lives of the people.

Although the Apidan theatre went through an artistic development of its own alongside the Egungun Society, it still retains a link to that Society. Formally, it continues to be part of the organisation, but a more important fact is that it shares the philosophical background and meaning of an Egungun masquerade.[6] An Egungun masquerade is regarded as the spirit of a deceased person or as the spirits of the ancesters collectively. Everybody knows, of course, that the garment conceals a human being, but he is invested with powers beyond his normal ability. Members of the Egungun Society invoke the ancestors to ask their blessing, help or guidance, and "the spirit of the ancestors is materialised in the *Egúngún*" (Awolalu 1979, 65). The Egungun Society, then, "takes care of the communal worship of the ancestors" and is "a mediator between the living and the dead" (Götrick 1984, 38). The appearance of an Egungun masquerade means the presence of a superhuman realm. And to various degrees this is also true of an Apidan masquerade.

The Ayelabola troupe

There are many Apidan troupes. Many more have existed, and new troupes are still being created. Many troupes have a long history. One of these troupes is Ayelabola in Ibadan. The name Ayélabóla means "we meet wealth in the world."[7] The troupe is inherited from father to son. A few years ago, its leader Ojedara (*òjè* connotes actor) generously shared his knowledge about the history of the troupe with me. I am also using the information given to Adedeji in 1965 by Ojeleke, who was then about 90 years old and the leader of the troupe (Adedeji 1969, *passim.*).

---

6. By "masquerade" I understand the Egungun costume and the man underneath it, when made into a unified whole by a superhuman power.

7. Ayelabola as a name of a troupe is not unique to the troupe described here. There was also a troupe with that name in Abeokuta, which later transferred to Lagos. Adedeji (1969, 350f) mentions an Ayelabola troupe in Imala, set up by an apprentice of the Abeokuta troupe. And he also says that there probably was an Ayelabola troupe in Old Oyo (1969, 319f).

The founder of the Ayelabola troupe was Imidiji, who later took the professional name of Ojediji. He hailed from Inisha[8] near Ikirun.[9] Ojediji was succeeded by his son Ojelade, under whose leadership the troupe also performed as entertainers and became the best in the area.

Once Ajeyi Oboriefon, who was the Balogun of Ibadan from 1871 to 1879, visited the Olokuku of Okuku and was entertained by Ojelade and his troupe. Ojedara says that Ojelade was only a small boy when the guests were arriving, but was already a grown-up man, when they reached the Olokuku's throne. This should be understood to mean that Ojelade only temporarily changed his appearance so as to look like a child. This was, then, one of his miracles, "idan." The Balogun was so impressed that he asked Ojelade to join the Ibadan forces against the Ijesha-Ekiti-Ilorin who were in revolt. According to Adedeji's information, Ojelade took part in the Jalumi War disguised as an *oyinbo*, white man. This stratagem made the enemies flee, since "they could not fight the ghost of a white man!" (Adedeji 1969, 322). Ojedara says that the members of the troupe were invulnerable. Thus they stretched their arms sideways, and the bullets shot at them were caught in the folds of their garments and fell to the ground. The bullets were collected and used to fire back at the enemies, who were then shot by their own bullets! Helped by these different means the Ibadan forces were victorious by the end of November 1878. Ojelade died and was succeeded by his son Olojede. Now Ayelabola was a purely entertaining troupe.

Ajayi Osungbekun, the new Balogun of Ibadan, asked the Ayelabola troupe to join the Ibadan forces again, this time against the Ekitiparapo. The performances were so fantastic, according to Ojedara, that even the enemies attended. They were mesmerized by the wonders, and so could easily be overpowered and taken captive. No wonder that, when the war was over in 1893, Olojede "was honoured as the best masque-dramaturge alive" (Adedeji 1969, 323) and made the head of all Apidan troupes. The troupe was invited to Ibadan as the first troupe to settle there permanently. Since then

---

8. Ojedara says that he hailed from Ikuku, which is also close to Ikirun.

9. Ojeleke told Adedeji that the troupe was created on the initiative of the Olowu of Owu, or rather on the initiative of a daughter of the Olowu. According to Ojedara, Ojediji, the first actor-dramaturge, founded a troupe of "fighting Egungun" by the name of Akukukeke.

Ayelabola has been recognized as the senior troupe in Ibadan and as such is granted certain privileges.

Initially though, the Ayelabola troupe met with some trouble in Ibadan. They came there about the same time as Capt. R.L. Bower, the first British resident, who arrived in December 1893. During the Egungun festival, Bower had some of the actors jailed, charged with disturbing the public peace. Olojede, of course, tried to intervene, but without success. Bower promised to release the jailed actors, only if the troupe could pass a test. The test was to prove, or—seen from Bower's point of view—rather disprove, a connection with the heavenly realm, claimed by the troupe. As a troupe belonging to the Egungun Society, Ayelabola too can mediate between the realm of the dead and that of the living, i.e. carry out a transition between the heavenly and earthly realms.

For the test, Bower ordered a big hole to be dug, a mat to be spread on the hole, and a chair to be put on the mat. Then he asked any member of the troupe to sit on the chair, but warned that if they fell into the pit, they would be buried alive in it. Olojede[10] tried to sit on the chair, but fell into the pit. Just as Bower warned, the pit was filled with sand, and Bower placed himself on a chair on top of the mound. Two actors made sacrifices though, and Olojede miraculously reappeared lifting Bower seated on his chair. Then Bower was forced to acknowledge Ayelabola's heavenly power. Since then, says Ojedara, the Ayelabola troupe has performed in Ibadan without any disturbance.

Whether real or fictional, this story brings out the basic idea of the Egungun Society, whose tasks are to bring back the dead in the shape of an Egungun masquerade to pay a last visit to the family; to honour the ancestors individually and collectively; and to mediate between the living and the dead. Most of these elements can be found in the incident told by Ojedara, namely a buried, and thus dead, person, who is brought back to life as a result of intervention by the Egungun Society. Through sacrifices two actors, i.e. the Egungun Society, ask the ancestors to prove their might over Bower. Help is granted and manifested by bringing Olojede out from under the earth, i.e. a resurrection. And the resurrection overturns Bower's

---

10. Ojedara attributes the event to Ojelade, the father of Olojede. According to Ojeleke (Adedeji, 1969, 179) however, Olojede was the leader of the Ayelabola troupe already during the Kiriji War (1879–1886), and so must have been the leader during the company's first years in Ibadan.

position on top of the grave, and so his symbol of victory becomes a symbol of false conclusion and defeat. In the end, then, Bower's test establishes Ayelabola's ability to invoke the ancestors and to make them intervene using the troupe as their agent. Olojede has proved his troupe a true representative of the Egungun Society. At the same time, he has proved himself a powerful magician and a good entertainer. Olojede was made the Baale, chief, of all actor-dramaturges of the Ibadan area. On his death, he was succeeded by his son Ojeleke, who was born about 1875, according to Adedeji (1969, 321).[11]

In 1976 when I first met the troupe, Ojedara, then about 55 years old with the private name of Fakayode, was the leader, the sixth since the founding of the troupe. He mentioned a brother of Ojeleke, a certain Ojewuyi, as his father and predecessor.[12] Ojedara has no formal education but has trained for many years in the actor's profession. He supports his family with the income from the Apidan troupe. And, like many Apidan actors, he is also a herbalist. This

---

11. Ojeleke must have been the leader for many years, probably from the early years of the 20th century and well into the 1960s. When interviewed by Adedeji in 1965, he was still the leader, and he was also the chairman of all Apidan troupes as well as the Alagba of the Egungun Society in Ibadan.

Ojeleke and Ojedara give exactly the same genealogy, but Ojedara attributes some events to one generation older than Ojeleke does. When calculating who is more likely to be correct, I have started from the very few dates given. In 1965, Adedeji estimates Ojeleke's age to be about 90 years, which sets his birth at about 1875. With a calculated span of roughly 25 years between the generations, Olojede would have been born about 1850, Ojelade about 1825, and Omidiji, the founder, about 1800. Following this calculation, the troupe would have come into existence not later than the second quarter of the 19th century. And this comes fairly close to Ojeleke's information to Adedeji that the founding took place after the Fulani attack on Owu and its subsequent sacking. The Fulani Jihad affected the Yoruba area from about 1817, and in 1835 Old Oyo was deserted. Sometime in between probably, Owu fell to the Fulani.

The information given by both Ojeleke and Ojedara makes a clear distinction between two occasions of participation in war. And the information forwarded by Adedeji refers to the various Ibadan Balogun, whose periods of office are known. If Ojedara's information about Omidiji's participation in the Jalumi War or the earliest phase of the Ekitiparapo War is correct, then it follows that Omidiji would have been about 75 years old—or even older—when going to war, which is highly unlikely. Therefore, I find Ojeleke's account of the history more likely to be correct, and I accept his statements that Ojelade was the leader in 1878, and Olojede during the Kiriji War.

12. In this context, "father" need not mean the biological father but the person from whom the office was inherited or handed over.

particular troupe does not employ the services of women at all. In other Apidan troupes, women perform the important function of singers or bards but never appear as actors.

Ojedara has trained several of his sons to be actors. Most of the training consists in observation of, and participation in the performances. Since the elder sons have other professions of their own, they cannot take part in every performance. When the company is asked to give important official perormances, for instance at the court, the most skilful sons are expected to come home to act. In less important performances the young sons of eight to fifteen, who are still being trained, are trusted with many roles. Even younger children, who show talent for acting, are given minor roles.

Like the leaders before him, Ojedara takes trainees from outside the family. After having paid an entrance fee, such a trainee lives as a member of the family with all its rights and obligations. If he wants to start a company of his own, when he is considered fully trained after some years, he has to obtain the consent of his teacher and pay him a recompense for the training and the right to perform certain dramas.[13]

Apidan aesthetics

The art of the actor rests basically on the mastery of certain dances, of certain texts and of improvisation. Dancing, particularly the ability correctly to interpret the drum rhythms and to "translate" them into steps, is emphasized.[14] Miming and dialogue are also stressed. An actor must have a repertoire of texts such as incantations and praise songs. Some texts are performed with special techniques which it requires long training to master. The actors must also have a repertoire of dramas, often with an improvised dialogue evolving

---

13. The Gbebolaja troupe in Ibadan was formed in the early 1920s, and the Eyeba troupe, also in Ibadan, was formed in the 1960s. Both leaders were former apprentices of Ojeleke Ayelabola.

14. Throughout a performance the bata drums are played. The drummers, usually four, are not part of the company but are hired for each performance. The bata orchestra is not paid a fixed price, but has a given share, 40–50 per cent, of the income from the performance. Ojedara says 40 per cent; Ayandele, his lead drummer, says 50 per cent. The variance may depend on a claim of superiority. This testifies to the importance of the bata music for a performance.

from a synopsis. In many dramas, only one role is taken by an actor, although the dramas require an interaction. Here spectators are expected to become co-actors, and so improvisation is necessary to provoke the participation of the audience and to make interaction possible. Since the degree and kind of audience participation is unpredictable, a good actor must be able to adjust to whatever response he is given, even to no response at all. The richer the audience participation is, the longer—and better—the performance becomes. Hence it is most important for the actor to render the content in such a way that it suits the occasion and the particular audience. Mastery of the art of improvisation is, then, essential to good acting. A consequence of this open structure of the dramas is that there is no need for long rehearsals before performances. It suffices to brush up the content of the dramas and the personalities of the characters.

The importance of the masks and costumes is also great, since they help in characterizing the role.

All Apidan troupes have a standing repertoire of dramas, most of them shared with other troupes and some of them of considerable age.[15] Since these dramas are well known to most adult spectators, it is the troupe's individual rendition that is of interest. The repertoire can be divided into three genres. Joel Adedeji has drawn our attention to the Yoruba names of two of them, namely *idán* and *èfè*.

Idán means miracle, wonder, and is a good name for a genre where the dramas are characterized by lack of role-playing and imitation. All Apidan performances are opened by the troupe leader performing in his capacity as a member of the religious Egungun Society. He is not imitating an Egungun masquerade, he *is* one. A metamorphosis has taken place, by which the actor is temporarily changed into a superhumanly supported power, mediating between the earthly and heavenly realms. The liminal actor is not conveying any fiction but is non-mimetic. The bata dance and acrobatics belong to the *idán* genre.

In the action of an *idán* drama, a superhuman presence is intended to be perceived, but this is not so in dramas of the *èfè* genre—*èfè* means joke. Ojedara Ayelabola would not agree with this statement without a qualification. He emphasizes that all dramas require

---

15. The drama about a white man, *Oyinbo*, for instance, was performed during Clapperton's visit to Old Oyo in 1826. Of course, the details vary a great deal over the years and among the troupes, since improvisation is a virtue.

idán—"that is why it is called Apidan theatre"—but the degree of *idán* differs. And, I would like to add, the kind of *idán* differs too. What is needed for an actor to change from one character into another is different from what is needed to change into a position where he has contact with superhuman powers, as is the case in the *idán* dramas. Ojedara maintains that an ability beyond that of the common man is needed to perform *èfè* as well as *idán*. Dramas about ethnic groups and social vices belong to the *èfè* genre.

The third genre—transition—falls between *idán* and *èfè*, as far as the superhuman presence is concerned, and is marked by ambivalence. This ambivalence is quite intentional, as we will see. Dramas belonging to this genre depict persons or situations connected with special powers, often magic.

All Apidan performances include several dramas drawn from all three genres. The order of the genres is fixed. First come one or more *idán* dramas, then at least one drama from the transition genre, and finally *èfè* dramas. This sequence can be multiplied in long performances. The arrangement of the sequence has its own significance. In the opening *idán* phase, a heavenly contact is established. The second phase shows a gradual return to the earthly realm, and so the ambivalence is meant to signify a state of transition, a state of "neither-nor" or "in-between," which also signifies an Egungun masquerade. In the third phase, the *èfè* phase, the result of the heavenly contact is shared with the earthly spectators. There is, then, a movement from non-mimesis to an emphasis on liminality, and from there to mimesis.

This sequential structure of a performance is the hallmark of the Apidan theatre in general. The individual companies have their own ways of handling this basic pattern. Good performances are marked by a multitude of dramas, and several repetitions of the basic sequence.

The artistic intention is also to present new and thrilling combinations of the well known dramas. The position of a certain drama in the overall pattern of a performance and in relation to the drama preceeding and following it, influences its meaning and significance, actually even its genre. For instance the drama about the white man acquires very different connotations, if it follows upon the drama about a pig or upon the drama about the god Shango. The Ayelabola company has an extensive repertoire of dramas, and Ojedara really knows how to make use of new combinations so as to give unexpected meanings to each drama, or, as it were, to reveal hidden truths about society and the human race.

In Nigeria, Apidan is far from being the only professional theatre. The Hausa Yankamanci and the Ijaw Owu plays, to name a few examples, are also performed by professional actors (Gidley 1967, Okwesa 1972 resp.).[16]

In most cases, however, theatre is not confined to professional actors. Instead, acting becomes a pastime, arranged whenever somebody feels like it. Thus, performances may take place several times a year, or with several years in between, depending on resources and circumstances. Again, the roles are acted by men only, and they usually belong to an age-group or a Society. The Okumkpa theatre of the Igbo people is a good example.[17]

Whereas the frequency of performances of the theatre dealt with so far is restricted only by resources such as recompense for the professional troupes, production costs and available spare time for the amateurs, there is another kind of theatre, which must be performed only as one part of a greater, regulated entity, usually a festival. And then the actors are not professionals, but chosen from among the members of the Society organizing the festival. The Yoruba Gelede is an example.

---

16. Among the Ijaw in the Delta in southern Nigeria, the Ekine or Sekiapu Society, producing the Owu plays, functions as a theatre guild and a theatre school. Boys bent on acting join a junior grade of the Ekine society, where they are trained by older actors. Later the most talented boys are allowed to join a senior grade. Only when they have passed a test are they allowed to perform as professionals in public performances (Okwesa 1972, 22, 45).

17. Simon Ottenberg (1975) reports that the Okumkpa plays of the Afikpo Igbo are organized by two men, called the leaders, who are not professionals, but who might have organized or helped in organizing a play before. After several months of preparations, such as composing the song texts, the leaders recruit actors from among all the young and middle-aged male villagers. Rehearsals are conducted daily for about two weeks, when songs are learned, dances practised and roles distributed and acted. To achieve "skill in imitation, satire, dance, and movement is very important," according to Ottenberg (1975, 140). No more than one or two performances are given of a production. During performances the leaders function as directors and interlocutors at the same time.

Gelede

According to Henry John Drewal and Margaret Thompson Drewal, the foremost scholars on Gelede, the aim of the Gelede Society is to placate and honour the women who are considered to "possess the secret of life" (1983, 8). To this end there is a yearly festival with one night and one afternoon performance.[18] During the night performance superhuman powers are addressed and a religious efficacy is intended, whereas the afternoon performance is primarily meant to entertain the present human audience by means of a number of independent dramas. Taken together, the two performances present non-mimetic as well as mimetic actions (Götrick 1992). Since the actors address superhuman powers through non-mimetic action, it follows that they are liminal.

Men join the Gelede Society in order to seek protection from the destructive qualities of women by enhancing the constructive or creative qualities of women. It is from among these regular members of the Society that the actors—or dancers, to use Drewals' word—are chosen. Some members are more skilful than others, and in some families the skill is developed to an extent where they are considered to have special rights and obligations to the Gelede festivals. Young boys are encouraged to imitate the performances of the adults. Regular rehearsals are held only at a few places (1983, 106). At festivals the young ones may be given some old masks and costumes to enact these roles as a kind of prologue or warming-up. The audience, as well as the mentors, keenly observe and criticize the actors-to-be. Where the performer's quality and skill are concerned, there is no difference in being a professional, an amateur or a trainee: the actor has to follow the pattern set by the genre, to execute the various enactments perfectly, and to achieve a high degree of impersonation. A trainee should aim at perfection in simple enactments, demonstrating the basics of the art only (1983, 29-33, 106–11).

In the Yoruba theatre, as in some other traditional African theatres engaging professional or amateur actors, education and entertainment are important functions. Both are perceived by means of aes-

---

18. Like the Apidan theatre, Gelede can also be performed whenever a reason is found, i.e. in addition to the yearly festival.

thetics. The social norms, ethics, and aesthetics are taught, often by satirizing violations of the norms.

The spectators know perfectly well that the roles are taken by actors, even when a topical drama is ridiculing an erring real person or is recreating a recent event. Although the spectators in their minds might substitute a character in a drama for a well-known citizen of the town, they do not take the actor to be that citizen. When an Apidan actor enacts a drunkard, the spectators perceive the actor as imitating the actions of a drunkard. The actor behaves *as if* drunk. The action is mimetic. The spectators adhere to a convention of perceiving certain activities in a way different from what they would have done, had those activities occurred in different circumstances. In other words, the demarcation between actual reality and the dramatic fiction is clear-cut. This coincides with the Western definition of theatre and with the Western art of acting.

And like his Western colleague, the Yoruba actor is one of the most important, or even the most important intermediary link between reality and fiction. The enactment is perceived as fiction by the means of his acting. The actor is perceived as part of the ongoing reality *and* as part of the fiction simultaneously. The actor provides the means of reaching beyond reality into the realm of fiction. In this capacity the actor is liminal because he is able to cross the boundary between two separate realms: reality and fiction. In this respect there is no difference between a Western actor and an actor in the traditional Yoruba theatre.

But the actor in the traditional Yoruba theatre is liminal in another sense, too, since he also crosses the boundary between the human realm and the superhuman realm. The superhuman realm is that of the forces, or powers, ruling the universe. According to many African systems of belief, the superhuman realm is impenetrable to most persons. Because there is a gulf of chaos separating the two realms, any attempt at bridging the gulf implies fighting the chaos. Only particularly strong and gifted persons are capable of daring such a venture and able to return safely. Mediation between the realms is necessary for human beings in order to partake in the superhuman knowledge and power and also in order to affect the power by supplication and sacrifice.

Some traditional African theatres, then, mediate between the human and superhuman realms, the actors being the mediators. This act of mediating is usually attributed to the religious functions of priests. In some religious rituals priests also perform mimetic actions. The latter performances are strictly regulated and the pattern does not allow improvisation. On the contrary, it is very important that the texts and the actions are correctly rendered. If not, it is taken as an answer in the negative by the powers addressed in the ritual.

The Obatala ritual

Joel A. Adedeji reports (1966, 1972) on the Obatala[19] festival among the Yoruba that it includes "a dramatic enactment showing a mock fight between a protagonist and an antagonist" (1972, 321). In a "ritual dance-drama" (1972, 329) the chief priest of the cult dedicated to the divinity Obatala "impersonates Obatala" (1966, 93) while another priest acts an antagonist. The antagonist attacks Obatala, who is soon overpowered and taken prisoner. The king, in front of whom the drama is performed, intervenes and releases Obatala.[20]

Many of the different versions of the Obatala myths relate a disagreement and a subsequent fight between Obatala and an adversary, resulting in Obatala being exiled or jailed. Through an intermediary the quarrel is settled and Obatala freed.

The drama described by Adedeji is a re-enactment of the myth. The priests take on the roles of Obatala and his aggressor and render a choreographic representation of their fight. This clearly makes it theatre. However, the fact that the drama is enacted as part of a religious ritual and that the actors are priests, made Westerners overlook its theatrical qualities. The performance is theatre as well as religious ritual. Although re-enacting Obatala's struggle, the priest-actors also perform an authentic action that is not representational. There are elements of uncertainty as to the outcome of the struggle: Obatala's aggressor might overcome Obatala, and Obatala might not agree to come back. The priest-actors are the visual signs of a battle that is actually fought on a different level of existence, i.e. between superhuman forces.[21]

---

19. Obatala is the Yoruba god of creation, but not the high god. Obatala creates the human being in the womb.

20. Similar kinds of mock fight are found in many festivals throughout West Africa.

21. After my presentation of this paper in Uppsala, Karin Barber generously shared her rich experience from the Okuku town. She compared the Obatala ritual with

The entire ritual is a way of appeasing the negative and destructive forces of existence. By means of sacrifice human beings, through the priests, try to achieve a balance between the positive and negative forces. In the drama the priests will find out whether or not the community will live in peace and harmony as a result of a balance achieved. The outcome of the drama, Obatala's return, is an announcement on the outcome of the superhuman struggle: the sacrifice is accepted, a balance has been reached and, thus, harmony will prevail for the year to come. And the announcement is taken to be an actual fact as opposed to fiction. What has been announced is going to come to pass in the future. In other words, the act is efficacious.

The priest-actor is instrumental in making the enactment efficacious. This is so because in his capacity as a priest the actor can reach beyond the limits of the human realm and gain access to the superhuman realm. When re-entering the human realm he communicates to his fellow men, the spectators, his experiences in the other realm. The content of the communication is not understood to be fictional. The priest-actor's liminality allows him to bring messages from one level of existence to another, messages such as requests performed as sacrifices and divine responses performed as drama.

By the spectators the Obatala drama is perceived on two different levels simultaneously: as a re-enactment of a past or mythical event *and* as an authentic answer given by superhuman powers. On both levels the priest-actor is liminal. On the one level he mediates between reality and fiction. The reality is what surrounds the performance and where the spectators are throughout the performance, and the fiction is the surface content of the drama, i.e. the re-enactment of the Obatala myth. On the other level, the actor mediates between the human and the superhuman realms, since on this level the

---

the yearly ritual in which the king of Okuku narrates the long line of preceding kings and their deeds. The narration is performed in the first person; the present king personifies all his predecessors. Like a masquerade he incarnates everybody. As Karin Barber pointed out, when every previous king is speaking through the present king, time and space change from here and now into an almost unlimited perspective. The past time of a previous king and the present time of the performance are perceived simultaneously by the spectators, who consequently also perceive the mimetic and the non-mimetic enactment simultaneously in the Olokuku ritual as well as in the Obatala ritual.

This phenomenon of temporal, spatial, and mimetic simultaneity is not exclusive to the theatre but is a well-known element in many rituals.

enactment is an answer to an earlier request posed as a sacrifice to the superhuman force.

On the fictional level the actor is liminal in the same sense as all other actors in the theatre all over the world. This I call "fictional liminality." On the other level the actor is liminal in the same sense as priests are liminal. This latter kind of liminality, which I call "religious liminality," is hardly shared by the actor in present-day Western theatre.

As we have seen, religious liminality is not restricted to actors in what is often called ritual theatre or ritual drama,[22] to which the Obatala drama belongs. Amateur actors, such as the Okumkpa actors, semi-professional actors, such as the Gelede actors, as well as professional actors, such as the Apidan actors, are, to various degrees, liminal in the dual sense. Although the Apidan theatre is usually classified as secular,[23] some of the independent and self-contained dramas of which a performance is composed are religious dramas similar to the Obatala drama. Some even lack the level of fiction altogether, and then the actor employs only the religious liminality, that is, his ability to reach into the superhuman realm. This latter fact means that some parts of an Apidan performance are not fictional at all but only religious—they are non-mimetic. The entire performance is, however, perceived as a piece of art, created and judged according to aesthetic rules. Although performing a religious act, the actor is also—and simultaneously—a creative theatre artist. By the right kind of audience[24] only an actor who is religiously liminal is found proper to perform a fictional drama. A spectator might accept an actor who is only fictionally liminal, but his aesthetic pleasure is greater, if the actor is religiously liminal as well.

The educational function of the performance, too, is far more effective, if the actor is doubly liminal. This is so because if the mes-

---

22. It is so called because the religious function dominates over other functions, such as aesthetics, education, and entertainment, but does not exclude them.

23. It is so called because the educational and entertaining functions dominate over the religious function.

24. The audience at an Apidan performance, for instance, is nowadays very heterogeneous. Some spectators have a traditional system of beliefs that is unaffected by Western ideas, while other spectators are highly westernized. In between these two opposite poles a variety of mixtures of the two world-views can be found. The religious liminality is probably not perceived by a westernized spectator.

sage taught by the performance is perceived as emanating from the superhuman realm, then it is more powerful than if it had come only from the human realm. If the actor is not perceived as religiously liminal, the message he is communicating is not taken to be supported by a superior power. And then a very important dimension of the message, and of the entire performance, is lost. When the actor is no longer perceived as being religiously liminal, it is not only the religious function of the performance that is lost, but also, to a considerable degree, the educational function. This has grave consequences, since it is through the educational function in particular that the theatre takes part in the making of society. Teaching the norms and values of the society, the traditional theatre actually is, or was, an important socializing factor. The loss of the religious and educational functions seriously limits the theatre's possibility of creating aesthetic pleasure in the spectators, since the complexity of the performance, also, is diminished. Theatre becomes plain entertainment without its former strong involvement in social affairs.

THE ACTOR IN THE MODERN THEATRE

In most cases the actor in the traditional African theatres is still doubly liminal. But what about his colleague in the modern African theatre? The "modern African actor" is an actor who is educated and trained according to systems inspired by the former colonial powers and who works with dramas written in colonial languages.[25] In many African countries, drama schools are parts of the universities. The formal, westernized schooling necessary for admission to a university drama school more often than not implies a sceptical stance towards a traditional African world-view. The traditional systems of beliefs are weakened by the Christian and Muslim religions, by Western natural sciences and general attitudes of superiority toward African philosophies. All this has affected the modern actor, who

---

25. For heuristic reasons I have chosen to analyse the opposite poles, as it were, and disregard all forms in between, that is the popular theatres such as the Yoruba travelling theatre. These composite forms of great variety were generated by the traditional and Western theatres and mostly have Yoruba as their mother tongue. The actors may be trained in the traditional theatres, or the modern theatre, or in both.

does not see himself as an instrument of superhuman forces, and thus does not consider himself religiously liminal.[26]

The traditional actor acquires his religious liminality partly through his training to become an actor, and partly by membership of religious societies. The Gelede theatre is performed only by actors who are members of the Gelede Society. It is, then, their membership of the religious society which allows them to become actors. The Apidan actors are members of the Egungun Society, the aim of which is to communicate with its ancestors. This aim can be fulfilled only by means of a religious liminality, and the Egungun members, including the Apidan actors, are invested with this religious liminality.

To become a modern actor, no membership of religious societies, traditional or otherwise, is required. Religious liminality is neither required, nor is it acquired by the training. In modern drama schools the two areas of activities, the theatre and religion, seem to be looked upon as separate, and thus the fictional liminality is attributed to the actor, and the religious liminality to the priest only.[27]

In modern African dramas there are, however, many references to religion and to religious rituals. In some dramas, religious rituals are even intended to be performed on stage. An interesting question is, whether these acts are meant to be perceived as fictional or efficacious. Judging from most critics and scholars, all parts of the dramas are understood to be fictional. Only a few would oppose this, but those few are the more interesting.

In his dissertation "The Idea of Tragic Form in Nigerian Drama Written in English" Atiboroko Uyovbukerhi presents a convincing and very useful theory of some traditional Nigerian theatres. As a contrast to the Aristotelian *mimesis* he uses the concept of *conjunction* to describe the meeting of three worlds, namely the spirit world, the material world, and the transitional world. Obviously Uyov-

---

26. So far, it has been correct to use the masculine pronoun only, since all actors in the traditional theatre are men. But the modern theatre has included actresses. It is not the liminal quality *per se* in the traditional theatre that excludes women, since some women, too, for instance priestesses, are liminal in the traditional culture. The implications and the problems involved when including actresses in the modern theatre are worth an investigation of their own.

27. Exceptions can be found in individual actors, of course, actors with one foot in each tradition. And a faint tendency towards an incorporation of traditional attitudes also where religion and liminality are concerned might be perceived.

bukerhi's theory accepts a theatrical enactment which goes beyond fiction. And it is the performer—the word preferred by Uyovbukerhi—who is the link between Man in the material world and the spirit world, and through whom the energy of the spirit world flows back to Man (1976, 86–140). According to Uyovbukerhi, the spirit world—or the superhuman realm, as I call it—is present not only in traditional performances but also in performances of modern dramas. I take his statement to imply that here, too, the actor is instrumental in conjoining the spirit world and the material world. And so the actor must be religiously liminial. But Uyovbukerhi speaks only of the dramatic form itself and does not really touch on other conditions needed by the actor to become instrumental in an act of conjoining, nor does he discuss the spectators' ability to perceive the conjunction.

Ijimere's "The Imprisonment of Obatala"

In order to better understand the problems involved, I will use a concrete example. A drama that lends itself to an analysis from the point of view of mimesis and liminality is Obotunde Ijimere's *The Imprisonment of Obatala*.[28] Mention was made above of the Obatala festival with a so called mock fight as an important feature, where a conflict between Obatala and his adversary is enacted by two priests. This mythical conflict, manifested yearly in the Obatala festival, is the basis of Ijimere's drama.

The content and the structure of the drama are fairly simple, as the following account will show. For ten years the two gods Obatala and Shango have not met, so Obatala decides to travel to his friend. The oracle warns, however, that Olodumare, the owner of Heaven, is demanding a penalty from Obatala for neglecting his duties, and that Eshu, the messenger god and mischief maker, will take advantage of the journey to mete out the penalty. But Obatala also learns that he "will thrive in suffering" (11), and so he decides to endure the suffering as his penalty, and he sets out.

---

28. In his *The Imprisonment of Obatala and Other Plays*, Heinemanns Educational Books, London, Ibadan, Nairobi, 1972 (1966). Obotunde Ijimere is the pen name for chief Ulli Beier, a German who lived among the Yoruba for a long time and whose knowledge and competence in the Yoruba language and culture is well documented.

On the road Obatala is repeatedly attacked by Eshu who tries to make him lose his temper by confusing his mind. But Obatala silently accepts the consequences of the confusion created. In the third attack Eshu makes Obatala catch Shango's favorite horse which seems to be straying. But Obatala is accused of stealing the horse, and Shango rashly sentences him to prison. Again Obatala accepts his suffering and trusts Eshu to turn "Wrong into right" (24) when the time is ripe. Against warnings Shango starts a war with Ogun, the god of war.

Ten years later the land lies devastated, not only by the ravages of war but also as a result of infertility. Ogun, bathing in blood, is pleased. Moved by his wife to seek the oracle's advice Shango is made to realize his rashness and releases Obatala, who declares that

> My suffering was not your doing.
> I had an account to settle
> With the God of fate. (36)

Ogun has to give up his bloodthirsty reign and acknowledge Obatala:

> Your reign has begun.
> Once more you have come to us to turn blood into children. (37)

And he concludes:

> Death and creation
> Cannot live too close together.
> Yet remember: They cannot live too far apart either. (38)

The universal conflict of the drama is that between creation and destruction represented by Obatala, the moulder of human beings, and Ogun, the god of war, respectively. The only solution to the eternal conflict lies in a balance between the two, a balance which has constantly to be renewed. In the drama this renewal is cyclic, and means that each power in turn reigns for a certain period. Thus in a cyclic movement the two opposites are made to be complementary, as Eshu confirms in the epilogue:

> The time will come when the owner of Heaven
> Will send me back to confuse the heads of men.
> /.../
> For if Obatala is the right arm of the owner of Heaven
> Ogun is his left arm. (43)

By pointing to the opposites and their delicate complementarity, the drama stresses the complexity inherent in existence as a unified whole. This is further stressed by emphasizing the complexity of the main characters. For instance Obatala, the god of creation, is not without faults: as a result of poor judgement and intemperance Obatala once created cripples. And this crime is the prerequisite for the conflict to take off. This crime also makes us aware of the risk that Obatala might once more fall victim to weakness, the result of which might be another disaster.

Ijimere has dramatized a material conveyed by myths and rituals. In the myths Obatala's struggle is continuous: over a long time he is repeatedly attacked, and he has to endure a long period of suffering. The Obatala ritual, however, does not show all the individual confrontations but metonymically chooses one which is thus made an apex of the ritual. It is at this truly pivotal point, if the enactment is perceived as a non-mimetic enactment, that it is made known by the superhuman powers whether the society is to have peace and prosperity in the year to come. On the verbal level the manuscript of *The Imprisonment* communicates far more than the traditional Obatala ritual. The traditional ritual relies on the competent spectators and participants already having the relevant knowledge about the myths, whereas Ijimere prefers to include this information in the dialogue. The competent participants in the ritual are supposed to be well aware of the uncertainty as to the outcome of the fight between Obatala and his aggressor at the pivotal point.

Ijimere too has tried to capture this uncertainty. In *The Imprisonment*, however, the uncertainty appears only on the fictional level, whereas in the traditional ritual it is, by actors and audience, understood to pertain to the actual outcome of the ritual in the sense that the decision is understood to be taken by superhuman powers.

As far as the relation between fiction and reality is concerned, the traditional Obatala ritual functions on two levels simultaneously, as pointed out above. On one level the priest-actors re-enact a mythical history of Obatala's struggle; and on another level the same enactment is perceived by competent participants as the visual manifestation of an actual fight going on on a superhuman level. The enactment is, then, perceived to be mimetic and non-mimetic at the same time, and the priest-actors are religiously as well as fictionally liminal.

This ambivalence cannot be achieved by a printed text, since a print cannot convey to a reader the impression that a superhuman power is involved in the act of reading so as to interfere with the outcome of the conflict. As printed, the text remains the same from reading to reading.

As a text to be read in a book, then, Ijimere's drama fails to achieve a conjunction of the spirit world, the material world and the transitional world, to use Uyovbukerhi's terminology. However, a written drama is not an end in itself, but rather a starting point for a theatre production. And the question is what the drama can do when performed on stage. Can *The Imprisonment*, performed by actors in front of an audience, give rise to the same effects as a performance of a ritual drama? What is needed to make the audience perceive the actors as religiously liminal and the enactments as non-mimetic?

As a manuscript, the drama possesses some of the prerequisites for a performance to achieve religious liminality since it is about conflicting superhuman powers meeting in pivotal points the outcome of which are portrayed as affecting humanity. But these prerequisites do not suffice. Prerequisites outside the drama are quite as essential. Some of these are the competence and expectations of the actors and the audience. The context of the event is also important.

In traditional ritual performances, many actors and spectators share in a system of codes, that is to say they have some competence in common and hence also some expectations as to the message and meaning of the performance. For instance, many spectators expect the actors to be able to communicate with superhuman powers. It is this *Vorverständnis* that makes the audience perceive a dual liminality in the enactment of the fight between Obatala and his aggressor in the ritual.

What general competence is shared among actors and audience of the modern theatre, to which *The Imprisonment* belongs in spite of its mythical subject? And to what extent does this competence include the *Vorverständnis* of the traditional ritual theatre? Are the audience expectations of the ritual theatre compatible with the modern theatre? An essential question is: can a god be addressed in a modern theatrical performance? None of these questions can be answered here. I will just try to indicate some of the problems involved in any attempt to answer them.

A crucial issue is the religious liminality. Since most actors in the modern theatre have a westernized schooling and are probably not members of any traditional religious society, I doubt that they look upon themselves as religiously liminal. Hence I find them more likely to imitate when religious rituals are to be enacted in a performance.

In Scene II of *The Imprisonment*, for instance, a priest "throws the palm-nuts and chants the ritual verse" (8), that is, he calls upon the oracle to announce the consequences of Obatala's journey to Shango. When a similar event takes place in reality, it is an act of religious dimensions. The message given through the priest is understood to come from the god of the oracle, and it is expected to foretell what will come to pass in the future. Performing *The Imprisonment* on stage, the actor, if he is not a priest himself, has to take on the role of the priest, which is to say that he has to imitate the actions of a priest. Imitating the religious liminality the actor crosses the border between reality and fiction only, rather than the border between the human and superhuman realms. The actor is fictionally liminal rather than religiously liminal.

But even so, some spectators might perceive the enactment as non-mimetic and the actor as religiously liminal. A prerequisite for this is, however, that the spectators' competence and expectations allow them to interpret the event in terms of religion as well as in terms of theatre.

A spectator with a traditional competence watching the priest on stage might apprehend the act as an authentic ritual (given that it is correctly executed). Such a spectator interprets the act as non-mimetic, and he expects the given answer to come from the oracle and to pertain to reality as opposed to the fiction of the drama.

But it probably takes more than the presence of a real priest on a modern stage for most traditionally oriented spectators to perceive the performance, or part of it, as a ritual.

If the actor really is a priest, the production has to decide whether he is to imitate or really to cast his *opele* in a true search for the god's answer. The essential question here is whether a god can be addressed and expected to respond in a modern theatrical performance. Since this question cannot be answered here, I will only indicate some areas of importance to the issue. One such area is the extent to which the properties of a traditional ritual can be changed into a modern performance and still create the same religious effect. Another area is the context of the event.

In *The Imprisonment* most roles are divinities, and it is open to doubt that such a constellation is acceptable as an efficacious ritual to a traditional spectator. In the ritual theatre corresponding roles— distributed in several dramas—would be taken by priests belonging to the respective cults of the different gods, and these priests seldom interact across their cults.

And further, will the rendition of these roles in accordance with the manuscript be accepted? The manuscript presents the mythic material in a way that is marked by the narrative form of the myths rather than by the demonstrational form of the ritual theatre. This verbal quality makes a performance deviate strongly from the set pattern of ritual.

The story itself is very different from the story enacted in the ritual theatre. In the ritual theatre there is only one truly pivotal point, whereas in *The Imprisonment* several such points are enacted.[29] As I see it, there is a risk that the enactment of several such events weaken the story line and also the possibility for each event to be seen as a moment for the superhuman realm to make its presence and decision known.

The perception and understanding of an audience with a traditional competence are likely to be affected by this kind of irregularities in relation to the traditional ritual theatre. Too many of the properties characterizing the ritual as a genre have been tampered with or are lacking. As a result, spectators might not recognize a performance of *The Imprisonment* as a ritual but attribute it to another genre. Then it would cease to be a ritual.

The entire theatrical event as such also differs radically from that of the ritual theatre. Modern theatre mostly makes use of modern theatre buildings and modern equipment. A production encompasses several, maybe many performances, probably given at any time of the year. But the ritual drama is performed as one part of a greater unified whole, where each part is essential to the efficiency of the whole. Preceded by strictly regulated religious rituals, the ritual drama must only be performed at the proper spot, usually a sacred place, at the proper time of the year, and in the presence of certain

---

29. The three escalating attacks on Obatala by Eshu enhance the verbal quality of the structure and make it resemble a tale rather than a ritual.

high ranking officials of the society. If any part were to be excluded or tampered with, it would jeopardize the entire ritual and what it is meant to achieve. In the modern theatre, however, each performance is its own unified whole, in which, for instance, none of the enactments necessary to precede a ritual drama are performed. The context of the modern performance differs so drastically from the traditional context that any attempt at perceiving it as religiously efficacious is likely to be adversely affected and even severely hampered.

Conclusion

Considering the fact that the audience in the modern theatre is most likely to be imbued with scepticism towards any traditional worldview, few spectators can be expected to perceive a religious ritual, performed on stage, as an authentic non-mimetic act of worship. The majority of the audience is likely to interpret the theatre according to the present Western theatre concept, which is based on the assumption that the content of the enactment is fictional only. In other words, the audience takes all enactments to be mimetic. This means that even in cases where the actor actually meets the prerequisites needed for a non-mimetic performance so as to create a religious liminality, a Western oriented audience perceives his action as fictional. Like its Western counterpart, this audience sees the performance as a recreation of the author's written drama. And so the spectators take the outcome of the story to be created and decided in advance by the playwright.

Since most modern actors do not mediate between the human and superhuman realms, and since it is commonly accepted by the modern audience that the stage-action is a recreation of a playwright's fictional story, it is tempting to conclude that the message of the performance is taken to emanate from the human realm only. And if so, the theatrical performance becomes just another personal statement like any other, lacking the enforcing power of a higher authority, as far as the message is concerned.

As hinted at above, the superhuman realm need not be understood literally as the abode of gods, but it can also be understood as the ultimate source of life and knowledge, i.e. the rules of the universe. In the traditional society it is the task of the priests and actors to explore this realm for the benefit of the community. But who is exploring this realm in the modern society? Many writers have claimed this to be their task. In some dramas for instance, the playwrights try to explore and communicate knowledge about the essence of human life and the position of human beings in the universe. This is often done by using some of the structures used by the traditional theatre (see Osofisan 1973, Irele 1981, 27–42, and Götrick 1984, 140–207). The authors' attempts make these dramas come very close to the aim of the traditional theatre. In both cases the aim is to communicate to the audience the highest cosmic knowledge gained by the dramatic creator.

In some respects, then, there seems to be a shift of the religious liminality. In the traditional theatre the *actor* crosses the border to a higher level of cosmic insight, whereas in the modern theatre it is the *playwright* who might try to do so. This shift has many implications for the theatre performances, implications which must pose quite a number of problems for the playwrights.

The crossing of the border to, and the participation in cosmic knowledge takes place here and now in the traditional performance, whereas in the modern theatre that crossing must be undertaken by the playwright before the performance. In the traditional theatre an actual, communal performance is even a prerequisite for the crossing, whereas in the modern theatre the crossing is undertaken in a private act by one individual—the author. In the traditional theatre the actor's seeking and obtaining knowledge *and* his sharing it with the society take place at the same theatrical event. In the modern theatre, however, this process is divided into separate events—the creation of the drama and the performance respectively. The drama is created as a result of the playwright's cosmic insight. And later, in a performance, the drama is re-created by actors and so shared with an audience, i.e. the society.

If some playwrights could be said to be modern counterparts to traditional actors as far as the religious liminality is concerned, then the modern actor becomes only instrumental in communicating the playwright's cosmic insight to an audience. The actor only re-creates this insight rather than acquiring it himself, and so he is fictionally liminal, since he mediates between the fiction of the drama and the reality of the audience. However, some spectators still experience participation in a cosmic truth, and the actor is instrumental in bringing this truth to them.

Bibliography

Adedeji, Joel A. 1966. "The Place of Drama in Yoruba Religious Observance," *Odu*, 3.1: 88–94.

Adedeji, Joel A. 1969. "The Alárìnjó Theatre: The Study of a Yoruba Theatrical Art from Its Earliest Beginnings to the Present Times." Unpubl. Ph.D. diss., University of Ibadan, Ibadan.

Adedeji, Joel A. 1970. "The Origin of the Yoruba Masque Theatre: The Use of Ifa Divination Corpus as Historical Evidence." *African Notes*, 6.1: 70–86.

Adedeji, Joel A. 1972. "Folklore and Yoruba Drama: Obàtálá as a Case Study," in Richard M. Dorson (ed.), *African Folklore*, Garden City, New York, 321–39.

Adedeji, Joel A. 1978. "'Alarinjo': The Traditional Yoruba Travelling Theatre." In Oyin Ogunba and Abiola Irele (eds.), *Theatre in Africa*. Ibadan, 27–51, reprinted in Yemi Ogunbiyi (ed.), *Drama and Theatre in Nigeria: A Critical Source Book*. Lagos, 1981, 221–47.

Awolalu, Joseph Omosade. 1979. *Yoruba Beliefs and Sacrificial Rites*. London.

Babayemi, S. O. 1980. *Egungun among the Oyo Yoruba*. Ibadan.

Brink, James T. 1980. "Organizing Satirical Comedy in Kote-tlon: Drama as a Communication Strategy among the Bamana of Mali." Unpubl. Ph. D. diss., Indiana University.

Clapperton, Hugh. 1829. *Journal of a Second Expedition into the Interior of Africa, from the Bight of Benin to Soccatoo*. London.

Drewal, Henry John and Margaret Thompson Drewal. 1983. *Gelede. Art and Female Power among the Yoruba*. Bloomington.

Gidley, C.G.B. 1967. "Yankamanci—the Craft of the Hausa Comedians," *African Language Studies*, 8: 52–81.

Götrick, Kacke. 1984. *Apidan Theatre and Modern Drama*. Stockholm.

Götrick, Kacke. 1992. "Egungun apidan—rituell teater," *Ritual & Performance*. Århus.

Ijimere, Obotunde. 1972 (1966). *The Imprisonment of Obatala and Other Plays*. London, Ibadan, Nairobi.

Irele, Abiola, 1981. "The Criticism of Modern African Literature," in Abiola Irele, *The African Experience in Literature and Ideology*. London, 27–42.

Johnson, Samuel. 1973 (1921). *The History of the Yorubas. From the Earliest Times to the Beginning of the British Protectorate*. Lagos.

Law, Robin. 1977. *The Oyo Empire c.1600–c.1836. A West African Imperialism in the Era of the Atlantic Slave Trade*. Oxford.

Okwesa, Fidelma U. 1972. "Traditional Theater in the Eastern Niger Delta of Nigeria as Depicted in the Owu Masked Plays." Unpubl. M.A. thesis, U.C.L.A.

Osofisan, Babafemi A. 1973. "The Origins of Drama in West Africa: A Study of the Development of Drama from the Traditional Forms to the Modern Theatre in English and French." Unpubl. Ph. D. diss., University of Ibadan.

Ottenberg, Simon. 1975. *Masked Rituals of Afikpo. The Context of an African Art*. Seattle and London.

Uyovbukerhi, Atiboroko S.A . 1976. "The Idea of Tragic Form in Nigerian Drama Written in English." Unpubl. Ph. D. diss., University of Wisconsin-Madison.

Historical Roots and Rural African Culture as Part of Bessie Head's Frame of Reference

Gillian Stead Eilersen

In 1982 Bessie Head, the South African born writer who lived in Botswana for almost half her life, wrote an article for the South African magazine in which she cast more light on the facts of her childhood than she had ever done before. She was an orphan half-breed, the daughter of a white mother and a black father. She said that the circumstances of her birth "seemed to make it necessary to obliterate all traces of a family history." She had no known relatives, no ancient family tree, not even "the sense of having inherited a temperament, a certain emotional instability or the shape of a finger-nail from a grandmother or great-grandmother." Then she stated: "I have always been just me, with no frame of reference to anything beyond myself."[1] In 1984 during a visit to Australia she said: "I just don't fit in and belong anywhere and I tend to pride myself on not fitting in and belonging."[2]

The second quotation especially suggests that Head had reconciled herself to this state of affairs. This is not borne out, however, by a closer examination of her writings. In fact it can be said that she struggled throughout her life to come to terms with her sense of alienation. Running as continuous threads through all her works are her attempts to confront this lack of a frame of reference on both a personal and social level and come to terms with it. My purpose here is therefore to examine the way in which she gradually does this in her writing.

Head's orphan state was dramatically aggravated as a result of the South African apartheid system. Not only was her personal background destroyed. She realised in later years that she totally lacked

---

1. C. Mackenzie, "Notes from a Quiet Backwater," ed. *Bessie* Head: *A Woman Alone* (London: Heinemann Educational Books, 1990) 3. Hereafter AWA.
2. A. Peek, "Bessie Head in Australia," *New Literature Review*, 14 (1985): 8.

any general measure by which she could appraise her own worth. She had no historical background:

> A sense of history was totally absent in me and it was as if, far back in history, thieves had stolen the land and were so anxious to cover up all traces of the theft that correspondingly, all traces of the true history have been obliterated. We did not know who or what we were, apart from objects of abuse and exploitation.[3]

Nor was she alone here. The same white men who had robbed her of her birthright had robbed her fellow Africans of theirs: "Most black South Africans suffer from a very broken sense of history," she wrote in 1982.[4]

Head was labelled "coloured" under the South African system. The story of her birth in the mental hospital to which her mother had been admitted, her childhood years as the foster daughter of a coloured family in the poor area of Pietermaritzburg, her subsequent mission school education and early years as a teacher and journalist is now common knowledge. But until she was thirteen, Bessie Amelia Emery as she was named, believed herself to be the daughter of Nellie Heathcote, her foster mother.

Then she was transferred to St Monica's Home, a mission school for coloured children. Here she was traumatically initiated into some of the main facts of her true background. This description is much quoted:

> The missionary opened a large file and looked at me with wild horror and said: "Your mother was insane. If you're not careful you'll get insane just like your mother. Your mother was a white woman. They had to lock her up as she was having a child by the stable boy, who was a native."[5]

It is not surprising that this passage from Head's third novel has been considered autobiographical. It is reproduced word for word in the *Drum* article already quoted which she wrote in 1982, ten years after writing the novel. Does this mean that she actually found her copy of *A Question of Power* and wrote out the passage? Or does it mean that the sentences churned round in her head like some endless gramophone record ready to be reproduced as needed? Though the

---

3. *AWA*, "Foreword to Sol Plaatje's *Native Life In South Africa*" 82.
4. *AWA*, "Social and Political Pressures that Shape Writing in Southern Africa" 66.
5. Bessie Head, *A Question of Power* (1973; London: Heinemann, 1974) 16.

The writer Bessie Head with her son Howard at the entrance to the Khama Memorial, the royal tombs of the Khama chiefs, Serowe, Botswana, in 1969.

protagonist of *A Question of Power* Elizabeth, need not be identical
with Bessie Emery, it seems natural to assume in the light of these
identical passages that Elizabeth's story has a highly autobiographical element; or that Bessie Head chose to give her later account of her
childhood a standardised biographical stamp. And an element of
melodrama. This does not mean that Head created a fictional family
romance and an "ideal biographical legend" to give herself the identity she longed for, as Susan Gardner has suggested;[6] and Gardner's
reasons for associating Head with hereditary madness detract considerably from any weight that could be given to her arguments.[7]
Records in Head's file at the mission school confirm that she re-
counted the details of her origins as accurately as she had been told
them by the headmistress of St Monica's Home and later by her foster mother. What gives these early biographical details a glow of in-
authenticity is the sad fact that Bessie Emery at the age of fourteen
misconstrued some of the most fateful hours of her life.

    In the *Drum* article, Head describes the events leading up to the
confrontation with the headmistress. She had been told curtly, when
the school holidays came round, that she would not be going back to
"that woman" because she was not her real mother:

> A teacher found me lying prostrate and at the point of collapse under a bush in
> the school garden. On asking what was the matter, I told her that I was about to
> die as no one would let me go home to my mother. Thereupon the principal
> bundled me into her car and for some strange reason raced straight to the
> Durban Magistrate's Court where a magistrate read something out to me in a
> quick gabble which I did not hear or understand. But he looked at me accus-
> ingly as though I were some criminal and said, hostilely: "Your mother was a
> white woman, do you hear?"[8]

It was on arriving back at the Home that she was told the further details quoted earlier.

    The extreme illogicality of these events makes them puzzling yet
provides the clue to their understanding. Too strange not to be true,
they represent a child's depiction of something which she had no
possibility of comprehending properly.

---

6. S. Gardner, "Production under Drought Conditions," *Africa Insight* 15.1 (1985).

7. T. Dovey, "A Question of Power: Susan Gardner's Biography *versus* Bessie
Head's Autobiography," *English in Africa* 16.1 (1989).

8. *AWA* 4.

Bessie Head believed herself to have been taken to court because she threw a tantrum. In fact the two events were not closely connected. Bessie *was not allowed to go home* because she had to appear in court. The records show[9] that eighteen months after Bessie Emery had started at St Monica's Home, the question of her maintenance came up for discussion. She had been left some money by her mother, and this was being used to pay a monthly school fee. But the bequest was small and it was decided to try to get Bessie declared "a child in need of care," thus making her eligible for government support under the Children's Act.[10] The remains of her inheritance could be kept for later years.

Correspondence concerning this plan began in July 1951 and continued until the court decision in the December of that year. So Bessie Emery was bundled into a car and taken off to court for her own good. The findings were that she *was* a child in need of care and she was placed in the custody of St Monica's Home. As from January 1952, a monthly grant of £2 10s was paid for her maintenance. In giving her version of this event, Head can hardly be accused of creating biographical legend. Rather this is an example of a shocking lack of communication between basically well-meaning people and a young girl in their care. The headmistress did not explain sufficiently to Bessie why she could not go home. She learnt of her family background in the intimidating setting of a court room. When the headmistress tried to talk to her about this afterwards, it was too late to save the situation. The emotional damage it caused Bessie is immeasurable. Her life formed itself in such a way that she could not later take this incident up for revision. It was locked away in a frightening compartment of her mind. Hence the rather nonchalant comments about needing no frame of reference. And hence the often stylised, mechanical repetition of facts about her childhood which her articles reveal.

Emotionally scarred, disillusioned, alone with a small boy after an unsuccessful marriage, Bessie Head decided to leave South Africa. She had trained as a teacher and then worked as a journalist and in March 1964 she acquired a teaching post in Serowe, Bechuanaland. Later she said that in South Africa she "had been unable to record"

---

9. Letters in possession of St Monica's School, Durban, South Africa, 17 August 1951, 9 September 1951, and 9 October 1951.

10. *Ibid.* Court Enquiry under Section 28, Order II: Rule 2 of Children's Act, No. 31 of 1937, Durban, 19 December 1951.

her life there "in any direct way ... the environment completely defeated me."[11] No wonder that she frequently emphasised her feeling
of fragmentation: "I have lived most of my life in shattered little
bits," she wrote in 1974, and added: "Somehow, here, the shattered
bits began to grow together."[12]

Head arrived in Serowe when the village still noticed a stranger
and in that environment she did attract attention. Though her brown
skin stamped her as coloured, she did not speak any African language; and she had a small child whom she pushed around in a
pushchair instead of carrying him on her back; but no husband. If the
villagers thought she was strange, she found village life equally be-
wildering. Though she had left a country so riddled with racial dis-
crimination that it had affected every aspect of her life, she had
nonetheless come from a world of intellectual stimulation and political involvement. She had left the highly urbanised life of a promising
journalist and budding writer.

But what was the society like to which she moved? Though the
country was in the grip of one of its chronically severe droughts,
which meant the many villagers were subsisting rather than living,
Serowe was very much the centre of political activity. It was the capital of the Bamangwato people and ethnic loyalties were very obvi-
ous.The village was still recovering from the traumatic conflict which
had split it in two when the paramount chief elect, Seretse Khama,
had married a white English woman. He had been prohibited from
ever assuming the chieftainship himself. However, in 1964, he was
preparing to let popular choice determine his future as a leader: he
had recently established the Botswana Democratic Party and was
preparing to stand for election when the country acquired independence two years later. As everyone knows, he was elected the country's first President in a landslide victory.

Another unexpected feature of the village scene was the presence
of idealistic young Peace Corps volunteers from foreign countries.
Two years before Bessie arrived in Serowe, an exiled South African
Patrick van Rensburg and his wife had started the project that was
soon to affect so many people in Serowe. Realizing the need for pro-
viding the youth with a relevant vocational education, van Rensburg
was in the process of building up his comprehensive self-help co-op-

---

11. *AWA*, "Some Notes on Novel Writing" 62.
12. *Ibid.*, "For Serowe A Village in Africa" 30.

erative project into what later became the Brigade and Boiteko movements and is today known as the Education with Production concept.

Head reacted to this environment on two levels. First of all, it inspired her to write. She described things in a direct and observant way. Her early articles are rich in interesting local colour. For example, in a very early piece, "The Green Tree," she refers to a hardy transplant to the village, the widely used succulent rubber hedge, and uses it as a symbol for that rare thing, a stranger, in this case a woman, who like the green tree is "quickly able to adapt" to the village way of life. However, people of this sort "are most to be feared for the adaptation is merely on the surface, like a mask, while underneath they are as new and as strange as ever."[13] This is typical of the way she began to use her surroundings: the observant eye preceding the penetrating comment.

Three years after settling in Botswana, Head had her first novel, *When Rain Clouds Gather*, published. Here she not only used the theme of change, of co-operation between whites and blacks on a village self-help project which was obviously inspired by her new life, but she showed in her use of imagery how much she had captured and understood of her environment. Her description of a Botswana sunrise illustrates the point:

> (H)ere the land was so flat, and the sunrise crept along the ground in long shafts of gold light. It kept pushing back the darkness that clung around the trees, and always the huge splash of gold was split into shafts by the tree. Suddenly the sun sprang clear of all entanglements, a single white pulsating ball, dashing out with one blow the last traces of the night.[14]

She describes the faint blue mists as shivering "like homeless dogs" and slyly creeping "into the hedged yard for a bit of warmth;"[15] she talks about a little girl walking "like a windblown leaf;"[16] about the old man, Dinorego's reasoning ability, always there, at the forefront, "like a cool waterfall on his thoughts."[17] The critics were delighted.

---

13. G.S. Eilersen, ed. *Bessie Head: Tales of Tenderness and Power* (Johannesburg: Ad Donker, 1989) 46. Hereafter TTP.

14. B. Head, *When Rain Clouds Gather* (London: Heinemann, 1972) 16.

15. *Ibid*. 140.

16. *Ibid*. 138.

17. *Ibid*. 85.

It would be simplifying things too much to infer that Head could only write so lyrically because she had begun to put down roots in the village. In fact, as her letters to Randolph Vigne[18] clearly show, there was a second level of reaction to her new environment. She felt frightened of, alienated from, even appalled by village custom. Being the individualist she was, she could not adapt to and be absorbed into the conservative village behaviour patterns. She antagonised people. She felt herself pursued and victimized. It was an unfortunate circle, aggravated by her own poverty and anxieties about being a refugee.

One senses this subterranean level, though it is not expressed in her second novel, *Maru* (1971). Here she examines the theme of racial prejudice in a bold and imaginative way. She takes as her heroine a Masarwa (or San) girl, Margaret Cadmore, educated and talented, who arrives to teach in a rural village in Botswana. One of her biting comments reads:

> And if the white man thought that Asians were a low filthy nation, Asians could still smile with relief—at least they were not Africans. And if the white man thought Africans were a low, filthy nation, Africans in Southern Africa could still smile—at least they were not Bushmen.[19]

The enigmatic love triangle and the story of the chief who renounces his position to marry the outcast girl is given an extra dimension when one realises that far from making use of the King Cophetua theme (as one critic has suggested),[20] she simply took the story from the situation in her own village. Had not Seretse Khama relinquished his chieftainship to marry the foreign woman of his choice? All she did was to give the plot an extra twist.

It was immediately after the publication of Maru that the smouldering furnace of horror that had been building up in Head's mind since she first heard the story of her true identity at the age of thirteen erupted in a nervous breakdown. Her third novel, *A Question of Power* (1974), the most autobiographical of all her works, depicts this in strange—at times surrealistic—images. Not nearly as well received as her previous novels, it has since often been called her best. It is

18. R. Vigne, ed. *A Gesture of Belonging Letters from Bessie Head, 1965-1979* (London: SA Writers, 1991).

19. B. Head, *Maru* (1971; London: Heinemann, 1972).

20. S. Gardner & P. Scott, *Bessie Head: A Bibliography* (Grahamstown: NELM, 1986) 7.

certainly her most difficult. Artistically at least, she seems to come to terms with herself and her past. She seems to emerge from the harrowing experience with greater insight and love. And her final sentences—"As she fell asleep she placed one soft hand over her land. It was a gesture of belonging"—suggest that she has found a frame of reference extending beyond herself.

Indeed, her next three works, forming in their own way as much of a trilogy as the first three had done, show that she deliberately put her personal concerns behind her and turned outward to the ordinary people of her community. She wrote a documentary account of the village and its people entitled *Serowe Village of The Rain Wind* (1981). Here she focussed on individuals, structuring her account around three great personalities who had shaped the village: Khama III, Tshekedi Khama and Patrick van Rensburg. In her eyes they were all the same kind of men: "They wanted to change the world. They had to make great gestures. Great gestures have an oceanic effect on society—they flood a whole town."[21]

The way Head arranges her material, historically around her three key figures yet thematically linking each period, gives *Serowe Village of The Rain Wind* a vitality and organic cohesion that lifts it far above a mere documentary report. And the oral history she collected for this work "spilled over" into two other books, *The Collector of Treasures* (1977), a collection of short stories dealing with the position of women in society and a historical novel, *A Bewitched Crossroad* (1984).

The Collector of Treasures is one of Head's finest achievements. With deceptive simplicity and seemingly dispassionate objectivity she covers in these short stories almost all the major themes of village life and explores the whole spectrum of human emotions. Through cross references, ambivalence and an ironic distance, she highlights the muddle and confusion that is life itself. Christian saints are contrasted with "Christian" vampires. Enlightened Christianity, logic and moral courage are tested against superstition and witchcraft. True love and wifely devotion, sexual promiscuity and emotional insecurity, female brashness and insensitivity are all examined. Often she flavours a story with her own wry brand of humour, as when the whole village gets to know Mma-Mompati's divorce oration on "God, the Church, the Bible, the Sick ... the Honour of an Honourable

---

21. B. Head, *Serowe Village of the Rain Wind* (Cape Town: David Philip, 1981) xv.

woman" off by heart because she repeats it "so often thereafter;"[22] or when Lekena, the witchdoctor, appalled at the strength of the evil spirits haunting Mma- Mabele exclaims: "We can never tell what will happen these days, now that we have independence."[23]

Running parallel with Head's interest in the community is her increasing interest in history. For this she could thank her discovery of Khama III. Her admiration for him is undisguised and she has done much to popularize his image. She admired him because he "fought battles of principle on all sides, against both white and black." Thirteen years after first reading about him she could still say: "There is a grandeur in Khama III that is seldom found in men in positions of power."[24] Though she had planned a historical novel with Khama III as the hero, when *A Bewitched Crossroad* finally appeared, he was delegated to a minor role. For she had expanded her scope to include the story of the scramble for Southern Africa in the nineteenth century, seen from the black man's point of view. In this her final work, as well as in a series of "historical tales"[25] written in the late seventies, she displays an unerring grasp of the essentials. She singles out the power seekers, black as well as white, and shows how human emotions such as greed and arrogance provide the explanation for most of the historical events of the time. She examines the Wars of Calamity (or Mfecane) and the havoc Shaka and later Mzilikazi caused, and then shows how the evil doings of the white men succeeding them on the historical scene were worse. Not simply because they were white, but because they were greedier, crueller and more scheming than the black leaders.

However, at the centre of the storm during those tumultuous year at the end of the last century, ordinary life still went on, ordinary decencies persisted. At the centre of the storm, Khama III and his Bamangwato nation survived: "The forces for the scramble for Africa passed through like a huge and destructive storm, but a storm that

---

22. B. Head, *The Collector of Treasures and Other Botswana Village Tales* (London: Heinemann, 1977) 15.

23. *Ibid*. 55.

24. B. Head, "Collecting Oral History," *Mwegi wa Dikgang*, Gaborone, Botswana, 23 March 1985, 6.

25. TTP, "Property" 65; "A Power Struggle" 72; "A Period of Darkness" 78; "The Lovers" 84.

passed on to other lands. It remained black man's country. It was a bewitched crossroad. Each day the sun rose on hallowed land."[26]

In contrast to the earlier writings, which had all grown out of Head's personal experiences or contacts in the village, *A Bewitched Crossroad* is a much more ambitious work, demanding a great deal of research and a clear sense of direction. It is interesting to note that she insisted on calling it a historical *novel*. She was passionately concerned with the fate of the individual and as her protagonist inadvertently caught up into these momentous events she chose an unknown chieftain of the Sebina clan, a small group of people who had attached themselves to the Bamangwato and enjoyed the protection of the enlightened Khama III. This device not only gives new life to dry historical facts, but it relates history as it should be related: as part of the African oral tradition.

Head's indignation at the whites' treatment of the blacks is highly evident, yet she concludes her work on a hopeful note. She blends tolerance and generosity with her outrage, incorporating both historically documented facts gleaned within the white western culture to which her mother beonged and the vitality of the tales and legends of her black father's oral tradition. This is her contribution to the "hopeful trend" she saw in African history and her "attempt to shape the future, which I hope will be one of dignity and compassion."[27]

Although Head died far too young, in April 1986, *A Bewitched Crossroad* represents a rounding off of her second series of writing. She had tried to work into and through the traumas of her childhood and youth; she had bravely examined the situation of an outcast in rural African society; she had demonstrated how a sense of history can heal an individual and unify a nation. Though she never personally became wholly integrated into her African village, partly because of her own strong individualism, in her writing she clearly showed that she had found her historical roots. Furthermore through her struggle to establish an identity for herself, she has also offered to all those who live on the continent of Africa the chance of a greater self-awareness and self-respect.

---

26. B. Head, *A Bewitched Crossroad* (Johannesburg: Ad Donker, 1984) 196.
27. *AWA*, "Some Notes on Novel Writing" 64.

Thomas Mofolo and Nelson Mandela on King Shaka and Dingane

Carl F. Hallencreutz

Local and international history can often be employed to articulate one's own cultural identity. Sometimes a reinterpretation of history can channel political protest and propaganda. In this chapter I will pursue such a dimension of contemporary African culture by contrasting the way in which the legacy of the two competing Zulu kings of the early 19th Century—Shaka and Dingane—has been explored in the moulding of cultural nationalism in Southern Africa.

Nelson Mandela and Dingane, the Hero

It is assumed that Nelson Mandela's speech for his defence at the National Court in Pretoria, in November 1962, marks a peak in modern African rhetoric. In a symbolically very loaded sequence, Mandela, presents his summary of early South African Resistance History. He refers to Dingane, king of the Zulus, and to Bambata, the leader of the last traditionalistic Zulu Rebellion from 1906 to 1908. From his own Xhosa people he highlights Hintsa, Makane and Ndlabe who resisted the continous pressures eastwards by the whites in Cape Province. From the peoples of the North he dwells particularly on Sekhukhuni.[1] What is particularly intriguing in this compendium of South African Resistance History is that Nelson Mandela does not mention King Shaka.

As we recall from South African history, King Shaka was the ambitious Empire builder of the Zulu people from 1816 to 1828. He was a military genius who expanded the rule of his people and also developed his army as a means of national integration. The war economy, however, increasingly exerted pressure on the Zulus and those related ethnic groups whom Shaka had brought into their fold. Local

---

1. N. Mandela, *No Easy Walk to Freedom* (London 1986) 147.

fear of King Shaka evolved. In 1828 time was ripe for local resistance to erupt. Dingane, Shaka's half brother killed King Shaka and emerged as the new Emperor of the Zulus.[2]

Even so, it is not primarily Dingane, the fratricide, that Mandela hails in his Resistance History. Instead his focus is on what happened in Zululand ten years after the death of Shaka. On December 16, 1838, the Battle of Blood River took place when Trekkboers emerged victorious in South African history for the first time. Dingane and his army were defeated.[3]

In the South Africa of Africaner Nationalism, December 16 has become a national day of celebration loaded with religious patriotism.[4] In a liberated, post-apartheid society, December 16 will be maintained as a national day of celebration though with very different symbolic significance. Its legacy of "Dingaan's Day" will be reinforced. Indeed it will be the Heroes Day of the New South Africa.[5] The recollections of Nelson Mandela's speech on the eve of his deportation to Robben Islands have informed this recognition of Dingaan's day among the exiled politicians of the ANC in Lusaka.[6]

Mandela's historical references to Dingane in 1962 are thus very significant. They are even more interesting when compared to contemporary emphases of the great Albert Luthuli.

Albert Luthuli's view of Shaka and Dingane

In his autobiography *Let My People Go* from 1962, the then ANC President, Albert Luthuli, too, looked back at the dramatic history of his people. He recognized the achievements of King Shaka as Empire builder and military strategist. Yet he admits that Shaka exceeded the limit. His tough rule bred critique from within his own army. Anti

---

2. See further J.D. Omer-Cooper, *The Zulu Aftermath. A Nineteenth Century Revolution in Bantu Africa* (Ibadan 1966) 19–42.

3. *Ibid.* 41f.

4. However, even after 1948 the legacy of December 16 as Dingaan's Day was preserved.

5. It is as such a Heroes Day that December 16 has been celebrated by South Africans in exile.

6. In 1987 I was able myself to celebrate December 16 in Lusaka, Zambia.

Shaka sentiments were cleverly exploited by Dingane.[7]

Summarizing the achievements of Dingane from 1828 to 1838, Luthuli strikes another note than Mandela. According to the ANC President, Dingane was a modernizer who also provided a local base for the emerging Christian Community among the Zulus and related peoples. Luthuli does not even mention the Battle of Blood River.[8]

This interpretation of Zulu history is not merely an innovation of Albert Luthuli. Instead, the ANC President follows in the footsteps of Magema M. Fuze, the first Zulu—and, indeed, Black—historian in the modern sense of the word.

The legacy of Magema Fuze

In Southern African intellectual history Magema Fuze emerges as one of Bishop Colenso's early converts. He also served as informant on traditional Zulu culture to the committed Bishop.[9] Later on Fuze presented himself as an independent historian. At the time of the Bambata Rebellion he was the tutor of the royal family of Dinuzulu. He then settled in Pietermaritzburg, where he published his *Abantu or The Black People and Whence They Came*.[10]

Fuze deliberately combines mythology and historical facts when he explores the riddle of King Shaka. Summarizing his account he affirms that Shaka

> ... came unexpectantly, and he arrived when Zulu power was not great in Zululand, being less than many other powers which were greater than it. He came and raised up the power of his people so that it became stronger than all others. ... It was a most astonishing feat. And yet it was the great announcement foretold by his great grandfather, Ndaba, that he alone would be a great king, far from his progeny would unexpectedly appear the one who would rule the whole of South Africa.[11]

Against this background Fuze hails Shaka as the great Empire

---

7. A. Luthuli, *Let My People Go* (London 1961).

8. *Ibid.* 12f.

9. Cf. J. Guy, *The Heretic 1814–1883. A Study of the Life of John William Colenso* (Pietermaritzburg 1983) 207–12.

10. M.M. Fuze, *The Black People and Whence They Came. A Zulu view*, transl. H. C. Lugg (Durban 1979).

11. *Ibid.* 58.

builder. He does paint, however, a dark picture of what he sees as increasingly appalling arrogance on the part of the Zulu king. Even so he does not wholeheartedly subscribe to the fratricide committed by Dingane.[12]

As part of his account, which draws on oral sources, Fuze also makes use of representative quotes from traditional Zulu royal praise poetry or *izibongo*.[13]

The evolution of the izibongo tradition

Early European visitors to Zululand such as Henry H. Fynn and Nathaniel Isaacs have recorded how both Shaka and Dingane encouraged the evolution of traditional Zulu oral poetry into an established element in their court ritual. As such *izibongo* were used both as political propaganda and as a means of facilitating national integration across ethnic boundaries.

The advanced *izibongo* of King Shaka has been coordinated into an exuberant piece of traditional Zulu praise poetry by J. L. Stuart and T. Cope.[14] From the court of Dingane two French missionaries, J. T. Arbousset and F. Daumas, have recorded an equally exuberant *izibongo* of Dingane.[15]

Izibongo, thus, is a feature of the fine arts in traditional Zulu society, which had been restructured into an ambitious Zulu empire. As such, however, the *izibongo* tradition is nothing static or inflexible. A comparison of Dingane's and Shaka's *izibongo* reflects certain differences in the political style and claims of the respective rulers. Their preferred poetic symbols differ.

Even so the major challenges to and changes in the traditional Zulu praise poetry came in the rebellion of Bambata, to whom even Nelson Mandela referred.[16] At that time traditionalist royal praise poets, i.e. *ibongi*, had to face the heartsearching question if the rule of

---

12. *Ibid.* 71f.

13. *Ibid.*

14. J.L. Stuart & T. Cope, *Zulu Praise Poetry* (Oxford 1979).

15. J.T. Arbousset & F. Daumas, *Relation d'un Voyage d'Exploration au Nord-Est de la Colonie de Bonne-Esperance* (Paris 1982).

16. See Mandela above. On the Bambata Rebellion, see further S. Marks, *Reluctant Rebellion, The 1906–8 Disturbances in Natal* (Oxford 1970).

King Shaka had definitely drawn to its close. In his most involved novel *Chaka*, the Sotho writer Thomas Mofolo gives such significant evidence.[17]

Thomas Mofolo, Chakiyana and Chaka

Thomas Mofolo of the Moira Mission in Lesotho wrote his *Chaka* around 1910. It was first published in 1925 and in English translation in 1931. It was translated anew and reinterpreted by the Sotho scholar Daniel Kunene in 1981.[18]

Collecting material for his major literary venture, Thomas Mofolo visited Natal on a bicycle after the Bambata Rebellion. Most likely he met Magema Fuze in Pietermaritzburg. In his novel Mofolo gives his theologically quite involved interpretation of the rise of the *izibongo* tradition.[19] He also records the *izibongo* of Chakiyana, son of Msambeti.[20]

Here Shaka's military achievements are summarized in loaded symbols like Fire of the dry tinder, Sky that thundered, Elephant that thunders etc. Even so there is a defaitistic tone in this *izibongo*. Chakiyana concludes:

> My mother's little one,
> climb on my back and let us go.
> Some others are already carried
> on their mother's backs.
> They are the ones of Mbuzo, the ones of Nsele
> They are the ones of Sichusa
> of Dingankoma
> Locust which was trapped
> with a spear at Malandela's
> Locust which from the very start
> soared ahead.[21]

Thomas Mofolo is well acquainted with the revision of the Shaka legacy after the defeat of Bambata when he wrote what has been called

---

17. T. Mofolo, *Chaka*, transl. D. Kunene (London 1981).

18. Cf. D. Kunene in *ibid*. xi–xiv.

19. *Ibid*. 115ff.

20. *Ibid*. 117–20.

21. *Ibid*. 119 (the Zulu Original) and 120.

the first modern novel in Africa. In his introduction to the modern edition of Mofolo's *Chaka*, Kunene reinforces this point and takes it a step further. He illustrates how well Mofolo employs traditional Sotho imagery when he interprets and portrays the evolution of King Shaka as a far-reaching African ruler. Kunene also explores the mythological repertoire which Mofolo makes use of when he presents the tragic fall of Shaka.[22]

The basic existential issue in the life of Shaka is presented as a necessary choice between Isanusi, the traditional *nganga* who promises power but who demands total surrender, and Noliwa, the daughter of Dingiswayo who represents life in its fullness. Shaka opts for Isanusi and in the end kills Noliwa. When the books are finally closed, however, Isanusi demands the final sacrifice, and there is no remission of sins at the grave of Shaka.[23]

The impact of Mofolo's Chaka

It is well established in African literary studies that Mofolo's *Chaka* has made a remarkable impact in Southern Africa as well as—via Leopold Senghor's reinterpretation—in French-speaking West Africa. The question is whether *The Return of Shaka*, by the Kenyan writer Meja Mwangi, draws on Mofolo's *Chaka* or whether he is inspired by Mazisi Kunene's great Zulu epic *Emperor Shaka the Great* from 1979. Since Bambata and Mofolo's *Chaka* there has of course been further development of the Shaka motif both among Zulu writers in exile and writers in South Africa.[24]

In their response to Mofolo's *Chaka*, Black intellectuals have questioned to what extent Isanusi should be interpreted primarily in psychological terms as Shaka's *alter ego* or whether a more mythological interpretation is more valid. Ezekiel Mphahlele opted for the first alternative, whilst, as we have already noted, Daniel Kunene thought the mythological option more relevant.[25]

---

22. Kunene in *ibid*. xiv–xix.

23. *Ibid*. 121–27 and 165–68; there is a reference to Noliwa (166).

24. As regards the new interest in Shaka by the South African public, the ambitious series on Shaka on South African TV in 1985 is of particular interest.

25. Cf. E. Mphahlele's comments on both Shaka and Chaka in his *The African Image* (New York 1974) 24, 206–10.

Another dimension in the pursuit of the Shaka tradition since the Bambata Rebellion and Mofolo's critical assessment of the Zulu king is the reassertion of the Shaka legacy by conscientious Zulu scholars. Benedict Vilakazi, Catholic poet and lecturer in Zulu at Witwatersrand University in Johannesburg, has, in a slightly romantic vein, tried to renew the *izibongo* tradition.[26]

There is an interesting line from B.W. Vilakazi's Zulu poetry in the 1940s to the exuberant Zulu epic *Emperor Shaka the Great* by the Zulu poet and at the same time the committed ANC politician Mazisi Kunene.[27] Here the tradition of royal praise poetry is fully employed in an ambitious attempt to reinterpret Zulu history as a means of cultural affirmation. Kunene's confidence in King Shaka is compelling.[28] His Epilogue takes on mythological dimensions, which transcend the frames of references of Magema Fuze. Kunene concludes:

He is an Ancestral Spirit
he cannot be stabbed.
Even now they sing his song.
They call his name.
They dance in the arena, listening
to the echoes of his epics.
Till the end of time—they
shall sing of him.
Till the end of time his
shield shall shelter the
hero from the winds.
And his children shall rise
like locusts.
They shall scatter the dust
of our enemies
They shall make our earth
free for the Palm Race.

Mazisi Kunene's *Emperor Shaka the Great* represents a peak in the ongoing reinterpretation of South African history. As such, it is significant evidence of how history is used as a means of articulating cultural identity among the Zulus and indeed, the Blacks. Compared

---

26. See further B.W. Vilakazi, *Zulu Horizons*, transl. F.L. Friedman (Pretoria 1973).

27. M. Kunene, *Emperor Shaka the Great. A Zulu Epic* (London 1979).

28. On Kunene's interpretative perspective and literary ambitions, see Preface, *ibid.* ix–xxx.

to Mandela's preference for Dingane, the Hero, Kunene, however, strikes a very different note. Given both Mandela's and Kunene's position in the leadership of the ANC we recognize a remarkable inclusiveness in the cultural policy of that nationalist movement. Even so there remains a sensitive political problem in the option for either Shaka or Dingane.

The sensitive political dimension

With his views on Dingane as the first hero in South African Resistance History, Nelson Mandela represents one position in contemporary reinterpretations of historical developments in Southern Africa. With their Zulu belonging, Albert Luthuli and, in a later generation, even more decidedly Mazisi Kunene represent another. From his Sotho starting points Thomas Mofolo developed a critique of King Shaka which places him somewhere between Luthuli and Mandela.

Gradually there has emerged a more explosive way of relating to the Shaka tradition in the ongoing search for a relevant articulation of one's own cultural identity. These attempts have been encouraged by the Zulu Romanticism of Benedict Vilakazi and attempts from the 1920s to develop a new form of a Zulu *Inkatha*.

Since the mid 1970s this more exclusivist attempt to affirm the legacy from King Shaka has become representative of the new Inkatha emerging around Mongosutho Buthelezi. Today he identifies himself with the symbolism and purpose of traditional Zulu praise poetry. For better or for worse within Inkatha Buthelezi is the target of the renwed *izibongo*.

Concluding reflections

There is thus a rich legacy from both Shaka and Dingane, which provides very different possibilities in the reinterpretation of both ethnic and wider national history as South Africa now moves towards a radically new phase in her historical evolution. A limited ethnic articulation of the militarily expansive role of Shaka reinforces the aggressive isolationism of Inkatha. A more modernist recognition of King Dingane as the first hero may however provide too limited terms of reference for a coherent national history.

In this chapter I have limited myself to a comparative study of two characteristic motifs in the ongoing reinterpretation of local and international history as a means of articulating cultural and national identity in South Africa. This approach has not allowed a more comprehensive analysis of the involved Zulu symbolism which makes Mofolo's and Mazisi Kunene's contrasting literary interpretations of King Shaka intriguing. Nor has it explored the sensitive social and personal preconditions for the fateful conflict between Inkatha and the ANC and within the leadership of these two movements.

Nadine Gordimer and "The South African Dilemma": The Case of Liz van Den Sandt in *The Late Bourgeois World*

Rose Petterson

If one defines "post-colonial" literature in narrow semantic terms as "a concern only with the national culture after the departure of the imperial power,"[1] it is doubtful whether this definition is applicable to the South African situation. For South African writers, there exists a state of affairs which, as Stephen Gray points out, is a condition where writers are "suspended between African historical moments that should have coincided: we are post-colonial beings, but still we are preindependent."[2] On the other hand when, for example, the term is defined as covering "all the culture affected by the imperial process from the moment of colonization to the present day,"[3] Ashcroft *et al.* succeed in pinpointing that aspect which is most discernible in much of South African literature written in English, what they deem the "continuity of preoccupations throughout the historical process initiated by European imperial aggression"(2). White writers such as Nadine Gordimer and André Brink, who write in English, have been producing what one can term a literature of dissent.[4] This literature, firmly rooted in the South African experience, shows little evidence of receiving sustenance from a foreign culture. The colonial experience is repeatedly rejected as being inapplicable to the South African context. André Brink refers to this situation as "the transition from colonialism to post-colonialism and the di-

---

1. Bill Ashcroft, Gareth Griffiths, and Helen Tiffin, *The Empire Writes Back* (London: Routledge 1989) 1.

2. Quoted in Margaret Lenta's article "Fictions of the Future," *English Academy Review* 5 (1988): 133.

3. Ashcroft *et al.* 2.

4. Ashcroft *et al.* refer in this respect to the situation as being one where " the racist politics of South African apartheid creates a political vortex into which much of the literature of the area, both black and white is drawn" (27).

chotomy between Europe and Africa."[5] Starting with her earliest fiction Nadine Gordimer maintains that "already I used the background of mine dumps and veld animals that was familiar to me, not the European one that provided my literary background, since there were no books about the world I knew."[6]

Thus, it appears to have been the prime preoccupation of certain white authors, such as for example Gordimer, to produce an indigenous literature which was deeply involved with the struggle against the oppression of individuals, and all the morbid forms this can take under apartheid. Njabulo Ndebele does not exaggerate when he says that: "the conflict has preoccupied the imagination of people almost to the total exclusion of other concerns."[7] On the other hand, black authors writing in English, and representing the majority of those trying to survive the pathologies and distortions wrought on them by a culture based solely on colour, have until the 1980s been silenced effectively by censorship. What Gordimer has referred to as the condition of being "Censored, banned and gagged."[8] Subsequently, increasing efforts towards liberation were mirrored in the literature of these authors. According to Andre Brink:

> ... the urgency—even the stridency—of much of this writing understandably increased as culture in general and literature in particular were exploited primarily as weapons in that struggle, subservient to political goals.[9]

In February 1990, with De Klerk's unbanning of the ANC, PAC and other political organizations forbidden since the end of the fifties and early sixties, gagging restrictions were lifted and many of those banned authors who previously could not have been quoted were taken off the banning lists. In her address to English PEN's interna-

---

5. André Brink, "After Apartheid: Six Writers Consider the Future for Literature in Their Native South Africa," *Times Literary Supplement*, 4–10 May 1990, 472.

6. Gordimer, "Leaving School—II," *London Magazine* 3, No 2, May 1963, 61.

7. In Ian Mayes, "Writing to Reclaim Stolen Lives," *The Guardian*, 10 May 1990.

8. Paul Rich points out that the establishment of legislation which restricted these authors not only resulted in the cultural and political isolation of the white writers, but also prevented the renaissance of black writing from becoming more than a short lived phenomenon; authors such as Peter Abrahams, Ezekiel Mphalele, Can Temba, Bloke Modisane, Tod Matshikiza and Mazisi Kunene were silenced through exile or in some cases death. "Tradition and Revolt in South African Fiction: The Novels of André Brink, Nadine Gordimer and J. M. Coetzee," *Journal of South African Studies* 9.1 (October 1982): 55.

9. Brink, "After Apartheid" 472.

tional Writer's Day in 1990, Gordimer refers to the present state of affairs as bringing about an atmosphere where: "information and ideas dammed up for at least three decades began to flow in a way we had forgotten."[10]

Any hope of change in South Africa re-awakens the debate about the role of the writer. For decades, writers used their writing as a weapon against those responsible for the repressive conditions under which they had to work. The time has now come for South African writers to be receptive to what authors, such as Gordimer, deem is the need for a new "vocabulary of life." For her, and for other authors such as Ezekiel Mphahlele, the writer must now "create a base for a leap ahead into the future." This, of course, is based on the premise that the writer "must be free." Lionel Abrahams refers to the dangers inherent in a situation where writers in South Africa, after having rid themselves of censorship from the right, could find themselves subject to censorship from the left. For these authors it is imperative, to quote Albie Sachs, an influential member of ANC, that "loyalty to the future regime should not tell us what to write."[11] Gordimer too emphasises that writing, as a part of the struggle for freedom, has now reached the stage where it needs "to come out of battledress." For her, the freedom of the writer has always been of prime importance, a point she has stressed many times through the years in interviews and essays.

In the effort to peel away the layers of concealment which are so much a part of her society, Nadine Gordimer has, through the years, subjected both herself and her society to an excruciatingly close examination in order to relay "life as it happens to be." For Gordimer this implies the writer's prerogative "to tell the truth as he sees it in his own words without being accused of letting the side down."[12] She has pointed out that this dilemma has preoccupied other authors before her and refers in particular to Turgenev whom she feels has dealt with this problem with great honesty. It is clearly Turgenev's example of depicting things as they are which has infused Gordimer's writing throughout, what she in fact herself described as, "his scrupulous reserve of the writer's freedom to reproduce truth

---

10. Gordimer, "Censorship and its Aftermath," Address to International PEN'S Writer's Day, 2 June 1990, *Index on Censorship* 7, 19 August 1990, 14.

11. Mayes, "Writing to Reclaim Stolen Lives."

12. Gordimer, "A Writer's Freedom," *English in Africa* 2.11 (1975): 47.

and reality of life, even if this truth does not coincide with his own sympathies."[13]

This stance has moved critics such as Stephen Clingman and Kelly Hewson, among others, to suggest that Gordimer's writing is best studied in the context of Georg Lukacs' definition of the European tradition of Critical Realism.[14] For Lukacs, Critical Realism is not to be regarded in the contemporary sense of "systematic documentation." The novel, in fact, "represented the encounter of a superior individual with a society unequal to his sense of possibility, his faith in a higher human destiny."[15] Lukacs holds, for example, that a great realist would, unhesitatingly, set aside his own prejudices and convictions in order to describe what he sees and not what we would "prefer" to see. He should display what Lukacs terms a "ruthlessness" towards his own world picture. Realists, according to Lukacs, have to take, as their point of departure, the most pressing, "burning" problems of a community since the immediate tribulations of the people stimulate their pathos as writers.[16] Gordimer clearly identifies with what Lukacs calls the "great issues of her time," in this case the struggle against apartheid – both as a member of her society and as an author. In her fiction, Gordimer has consistently attempted to criticise sincerely her own *Weltanschauung* and has striven to render with verity the characters on her side of the struggle; their weak as well as their strong points. For her, the decision to be sincere has always been an artistic one, one she says she has faced repeatedly in her work and one upon which she remains adamant:

> As a writer I feel my first duty is integrity as an artist. I have a superstitious notion that if I lie, my characters will be damaged, somehow; their verity will be destroyed. I am making that kind of decision all the time, while knowing that I'm writing something that would be criticized and regarded as disloyal by the people on whose side I am.[17]

---

13. Gordimer, "A Writer's Freedom" 47.

14. In an essay on "Modern African Writing," Gordimer herself has said: "There seems to me no doubt that African English literature's best writers are critical realists."

15. Alfred Kazin, Introduction, *Studies in European Realism*, by Georg Lukacs (New York: Grosset and Dunlap, 1964) vi.

16. Lukacs, *Realism* 12.

17. Robert Boyers, Clark Blaise, Terence Diggory, and Jordan Elgrably, "A Conversation with Nadine Gordimer," *Salmagundi* 62 (1984): 5.

In demanding that writers be given total freedom in their quest to provide the world with "a deep, intense, private view" of conditions as they exist in their society, Gordimer has always exacted "freedom from the public conformity of political interpretation, morals and tastes" and has stressed that writers are entitled to this freedom if they are to go about their writing according to their best ability. The South African way of life has always posed its own particular problems to those who live and work under its restrictions:

> The private view always has been and always will be a source of fear and anger to proponents of a way of life, such as the white man's in South Africa, that does not bear looking at except in the light of a special self-justificatory doctrine.[18]

Thus, together with the threat of having their books banned in a country where political freedom was denied, Gordimer has, in the past, identified another less obvious yet more insidious threat as far as writers in South Africa are concerned. Stemming from their opposition to this denial of political freedom, the freedom of a writer's "private view of life," could, paradoxically, be threatened by the knowledge of "WHAT IS EXPECTED OF HIM."[19] She regards this as often being the demand to conform to "an orthodoxy of opposition." Her contention is that people might demand of writers that they act as their mouthpiece since they regard them as fellow-beings who share their ideals and their cause. Such loyalties and identification can be the cause of deep conflict as writers grapple with their conscience when integrity demands that they pit everything in the struggle "on the side of free men." For Gordimer this is a pitfall and she offers a dire warning to the writer: "His integrity as a writer goes the moment he begins to write what he ought to write."[20]

This need to assert the writer's "private view of life" is illustrated in *The Late Bourgeois World* (1966), which takes its title from Ernst Fisher's book *The Necessity of Art*, Gordimer created a character which, like Turgenev's character Bazarov in *Fathers and Sons*, is presented with "all the faults and contradictions that Turgenev saw in

---

18. Gordimer, "Writer's Freedom" 45.
19. Gordimer, "Writer's Freedom" 46.
20. Gordimer, "Writer's Freedom" 46.

his own type, in himself ...."[21] When Turgenev published this novel in 1862 it was attacked from both sides. The right accused him of pandering to the revolutionary nihilists, and the followers of the left, especially the younger generation, upon whom the character of Bazarov was modelled, bitterly attacked him accusing him of being a traitor to the cause. In his own defence, Turgenev made it quite clear that the character of Bazarov was based on observations of people like himself and was not created out of the need to insult anybody. Turgenev insisted that his own personal predilections had nothing to do with this depiction. He was motivated by the pleasure "which consists of castigating oneself and one's faults in the imaginary characters one depicts."[22]

Gordimer's "flawed" character, Liz Van Den Sandt, is the protagonist and first person narrator of *The Late Bourgeois World*. As she relates the facts of her life we are allowed to view events entirely from her own viewpoint, thus establishing an illusion of reality which is unsettling and particularly persuasive. Gordimer's technique although having the distinct disadvantage of restricting the reader to that which the protagonist-narrator could reasonably have seen, heard or experienced, nevertheless opens up a myriad of positive possibilities since it allows complete access to the protagonists thoughts and feelings. In gaining such access to Liz's thoughts and attitudes, we witness, from the inside, the debilitating and warping effects of a repressive system. We see clearly "the social distortions, the psychological distortion of apartheid"[23] as it effects the personality. Nadine Gordimer has said the following about the novel:

> My short novel *The Late Bourgeois World* was an attempt to look into the specific character of the social climate that produced the wave of young white saboteurs in 1963–64. I tried to follow the threads of observation and intuition back, through individual lives, to examine how this tragedy might have come about. As an artist, I am not concerned with propaganda and my characters were shown in all their human weaknesses. What interested me was not to "prove" anything, but to explore the interaction of character and situation in private and personal lives. What emerged from the book was the guilt of white society to

---

21. Gordimer, "Writer's Freedom" 48.

22. Quoted by Gordimer in "Writer's Freedom" 48.

23. Quoted by Sammy Adelman in "Nadine Gordimer: Woman of Fiery Conviction," *Wits Student* (Johannesburg), 19 October 1979, 18.

ward its own sons, who are, by its own definition, its failures: those sons who, if they won't act as white men for white men, are not allowed to act at all.[24]

The use by Gordimer, in this novel, of the point of view of a first person narrator has been questioned by critics but, as Diana Cooper-Clark pointed out in an interview with Gordimer, Liz's limitation is a lucid reflection of "the problems of self and the society she lives in."[25] Gordimer's point emerges with increasing clarity: no one in South Africa, even those who are committed, can escape the process of being "pressed and shaped from the moment we're born by the strongest possible political forces."[26]

In creating the character of Liz, with all the contradictions and ambivalences apparent in her personality, Gordimer adheres to an aspect of Lukacsian realism which is characterised by a "three dimensionality" and "allroundness" and which represents man and society as complementing entities rather than displaying certain aspects of either in isolation. At work here is the central criterion of Lukacsian realism, "a peculiar synthesis which organically binds together the particular both in character and in situations,"[27] and which constitutes the "type."

True to the definition of the Lukacsian "type," Gordimer's character, in that she rejects the South African apartheid system which denies basic human rights, can be regarded as displaying "the conscious view and larger vision that lead to a new society."[28] The "type" does not imply a stereotype, it is not the average quality which makes the type nor its "mere individual being" even if it is skilfully conceived. What constitutes a type according to Lukacs:

> ... is that in it all the humanly and socially essential determinants are present on their highest level of development, in the ultimate unfolding of the possibilities latent in them, in extreme presentation of their extremes, rendering concrete the peaks and limits of men and epochs.[29]

As a "type," Liz is the emerging white South African revolutionary in whose personality traits of detachment and self deception should

---

24. Michael Wade, *Nadine Gordimer* (London: Evans Brothers Ltd., 1978) 109.

25. Diana Cooper-Clark, "The Clash: An Interview With Nadine Gordimer," *The London Magazine*, February 1983, 57.

26. Adelman, "Nadine Gordimer: Woman of Fiery Conviction" 18.

27. Lukacs, *Realism* 6.

28. Alfred Kazin, Introduction, *Studies in European Realism* vi.

29. Lukacs 6.

be seen as the products of a divisive and repressive society. Here, in this novel, Gordimer illustrates how inextricably the public and private are intertwined. In Lukacsian terms formulated as follows:

> ... every action, thought and emotion of human beings is inseparably bound up with the life and struggles of the community, i.e., with politics; whether the humans themselves are conscious of this, unconscious of it or even trying to escape from it, objectively their actions, thoughts and emotions nevertheless spring from and run into politics.[30]

The character of Liz Van Den Sandt, in that it has been shaped and distorted by a particular ideology, appears to bring about a certain discord in Gordimer's text. The discord between what seems to be the consciously planned scheme on the one hand and the insistence of the unconscious which stubbornly disrupts on the other, acting as a prevailing reminder of how the repressed keeps returning.

Despite Gordimer's claims that *The Late Bourgeois World* was not concerned with "propaganda" but rather with the need to reveal all the characters' "human weaknesses," there nevertheless is a certain propagandistic standard hypothesized in the novel. How, in the form for example, is one otherwise made aware of Liz's bias? Gordimer exercises what she terms the writer's "prerogative" in an attempt at rendering the "truth" as she perceives it, thereby running the risk of being accused of "letting the side down."[31] The result, in her text, is a peculiar confusion of "objective" truth with subjective, political engagement. Does the typifying of character not suggest that there is a literary politics involved in the narrative? The novel raises the question of what would count as valid political action and, following on this, is the making of this novel valid political action? If one accepts the premise that, as Fredric Jameson maintains, the individual literary work is a socially "symbolic act," then:

> ... ideology is not something which informs or invests symbolic production; rather the aesthetic act is itself ideological, and the production of aesthetic or narrative form is to be seen as an ideological act in its own right with the function of inventing imaginary or formal "solutions" to unresolvable social contradictions.[32]

---

30. Lukacs 9.

31. Gordimer, "A Writer's Freedom" 47.

32. Fredric Jameson, *The Political Unconscious* (London and New York: Routledge 1981) 79.

About the Contributors

Lars-Gunnar Andersson is a lecturer in Linguistics at the University of Gothenburg. He is co-author of *Logic in Linguistics*, Cambridge UP 1977, and *Bad Language*, Blackwells 1990. Lars-Gunnar Andersson and Tore Janson work on a book about the language situation in Botswana; their project is supported by SAREC.

Hilde Arntsen is a graduate student at the Department of Media and Communication, University of Oslo. Her thesis is on the USA electronic church in Zimbabwe.

Olof Axelsson is a graduate student at the Department of Musicology, Lund University. He was Director of Kwanongoma College of Music from 1972 to 1982.

Ingrid Björkman is Associate Professor of Literature. For the last ten years she has been involved in development research. Her book on the role of indigenous people's theatre in Kenyan political development, *"Mother Sing for Me,"* was published by Zed Books, 1989.

Gillian Stead Eilersen is a lecturer at the English Department at Odense University, Denmark. She has recently completed a bibliography of Bessie Head, called *People Without Names: A Biography of Bessie Head.*

Bodil Folke Frederiksen teaches culture and development at the Centre for International Development Studies, Roskilde University and she is finishing a project on "Urban Literature in Kenya, 1960–1988."

Raoul Granqvist is Associate Professor of English Literature at Umeå University; he is a critic of African literature and is currently working on a project on African popular culture.

Kacke Götrick is Associate Professor of Theatre Studies at Oslo University, Norway, where she currently teaches African theatre.

Carl F. Hallencreutz is Professor of Studies of Mission at Uppsala University. From 1985 to 1988 he was Professor of Religious Studies, University of Zimbabwe, Harare. Previous publications include *Dialogue and Community. Ecumenical Issues in Inter-Religious Relationships* (1977); together with A.M. Moyo, *Church and State in Zimbabwe 1965–1985* (1988); and with Mai Palmberg, *Religion and Politics in Southern Africa* (1991).

Chenjerai Hove is a Zimbabwean writer, editor and poet. His works include *Up in Arms, Red Hills of Home*, and the novel *Bones*.

Tore Janson is Professor of Latin at the University of Gothenburg. He is co-author of a book on the development of Setswana, *Birth of a National Language*, Heinemann Botswana 1991.

Knut Lundby is a senior lecturer at the Department of Media and Communication, University of Oslo, specializing in the sociology of religion. Thesis subject: the collectivity of faith.

Adewale Maja-Pearce lives in London. He is African editor of *Index of Censorship* and a writer of books such as *In My Father's Country: A Nigerian Journey* (1987) and *How Many Miles to Babylon? An Essay* (1990), and editor of *The Heinemann Book of African Poetry in English* (1990).

Rose Petterson is a graduate student at the Department of English, Uppsala University. Thesis subject: Nadine Gordimer.

Karin Ådahl is Associate Professor of the History of Art at Uppsala University. She is currently working on a project on Islamic art.

Seminar Proceedings
from the Scandinavian Institute of African Studies

1. *Soviet Bloc, China and Africa*. Eds. Sven Hamrell and C.G. Widstrand. 173 pp. Uppsala 1964. (Out-of-print)
2. *Development and Adult Education in Africa*. Ed. C.G. Widstrand. 97 pp. Uppsala 1965. (Out-of-print)
3. *Refugee Problems in Africa*. Ed. Sven Hamrell. 123 pp. Uppsala 1967. SEK 30,-
4. *The Writer in Modern Africa*. Ed. Per Wästberg. 123 pp. Uppsala 1968. SEK 30,-
5. *African Boundary Problems*. Ed. C.G. Widstrand. 202 pp. Uppsala 1969. SEK 30,-
6. *Cooperatives and Rural Development in East Africa*. Ed. C.G. Widstrand. 271 pp. Uppsala 1970. (Out-of-print)
7. *Reporting Africa*. Ed. Olav Stokke. 223 pp. Uppsala 1971. SEK 30,-
8. *African Cooperatives and Efficiency*. Ed. C.G. Widstrand. 239 pp. Uppsala 1972. SEK 60,-
9. *Land-locked Countries of Africa*. Ed. Zdenek Cervenka. 368 pp. Uppsala 1973. SEK 80,-
10. *Multinational Firms in Africa*. Ed. C.G. Widstrand. With an introduction by Samir Amin. 425 pp. Uppsala 1975. (Out-of-print)
11. *African Refugees and the Law*. Eds. Göran Melander and Peter Nobel. 98 pp. Uppsala 1978. SEK 50,-
12. *Problems of Socialist Orientation in Africa*. Ed. Mai Palmberg. 243 pp. Uppsala 1978 (Out-of-print)
13. *Canada, Scandinavia and Southern Africa*. Eds. D. Anglin, T. Shaw and C.G. Widstrand. 190 pp. Uppsala 1978. SEK 70,-
14. *South-South Relations in a Changing World Order*. Ed. Jerker Carlsson. 166 pp. Uppsala 1982. SEK 90,-
15. *Recession in Africa*. Ed. Jerker Carlsson. 203 pp. Uppsala 1983. SEK 95,-
16. *Land Management and Survival*. Ed. Anders Hjort. 148 pp. Uppsala 1985. SEK 100,-
17. *Religion, Development and African Identity*. Ed. Kirsten Holst Petersen. 164 pp. Uppsala 1987. SEK 110,-

18. *The IMF and the World Bank in Africa: Conditionality, Impact and Alternatives.* Ed. Kjell J. Havnevik. 179 pp. Uppsala 1987. SEK 110,-
19. *Refugees and Development in Africa.* Ed. Peter Nobel. 120 pp. Uppsala 1987. SEK 110,-
20. *Criticism and Ideology. Second African Writers' Conference—Stockholm 1986.* Ed. Kirsten Holst Petersen. 221 pp. Uppsala 1988. SEK 150,-
21. *Cooperatives Revisited.* Ed. Hans Hedlund. 223 pp. Uppsala 1988. SEK 170,-
22. *Regional Cooperation in Southern Africa. A Post–Apartheid Perspective.* Eds. Bertil Odén and Haroub Othman. 243 pp. Uppsala 1989. SEK 170,-
23. *Small Town Africa. Studies in Rural–Urban Interaction.* Ed. Johathan Baker. 268 pp. Uppsala 1990. SEK 170,-
24. *Religion and Politics in Southern Africa.* Eds. Carl Fredrik Hallencreutz and Mai Palmberg. 219 pp. Uppsala 1991. SEK 170.-
25. *When the Grass is Gone. Development Intervention in African Arid Lands.* Ed. P.T.W. Baxter. 215 pp. Uppsala 1991. SEK 170,-
26. *Authoritarianism, Democracy and Adjustment. The Politics of Economic Reform in Africa.* Eds. Peter Gibbon, Yusuf Bangura and Arve Ofstad. 236 pp. Uppsala 1992. SEK 230,- (hard cover), SEK 145,- (soft cover)
27. *The Rural–Urban Interface in Africa. Expansion and Adaptation.* Eds. Jonathan Baker and Poul Ove Pedersen. pp. Uppsala 1992. SEK 230,- (hard cover), SEK 145,- (soft cover)
28. *Southern Africa after Apartheid. Regional Integration and External Resources.* Ed. Bertil Odén. 279 pp. Uppsala 1993. SEK 200,-
29. *Culture in Africa. An Appeal for Pluralism.* Ed. Raoul Granqvist. 206 pp. Uppsala 1993. SEK 200,-